ACCOLADES

A WOMEN WHO SUBMIT ANTHOLOGY

MANAGING & FICTION EDITORS

Tisha Marie Reichle-Aguilera
Rachael Warecki

NONFICTION EDITORS

Ryane Nicole Granados
Noriko Nakada
Ashley Perez

POETRY EDITORS

Xochitl-Julisa Bermejo
Lauren Eggert-Crowe

FOUNDERS

Alyss Dixson
Ashaki Jackson
Xochitl-Julisa Bermejo

Accolades: A Women Who Submit Anthology

Jamii Publishing

Copyright ©2020 Women Who Submit

All rights reserved.

Jamii Publishing
Santa Cruz, CA
www.jamiipublishing.com
[clmp]

Cover Design & Photo: Rachael Warecki
Text Design: Rachael Warecki
Managing Editors: Tisha Marie Reichle-Aguilera and
Rachael Warecki
Production: Nikia Chaney, Cynthia Manick, Emily Blair

Library of Congress Cataloging-in-Publishing Data

ISBN: 978-1-7332415-2-6

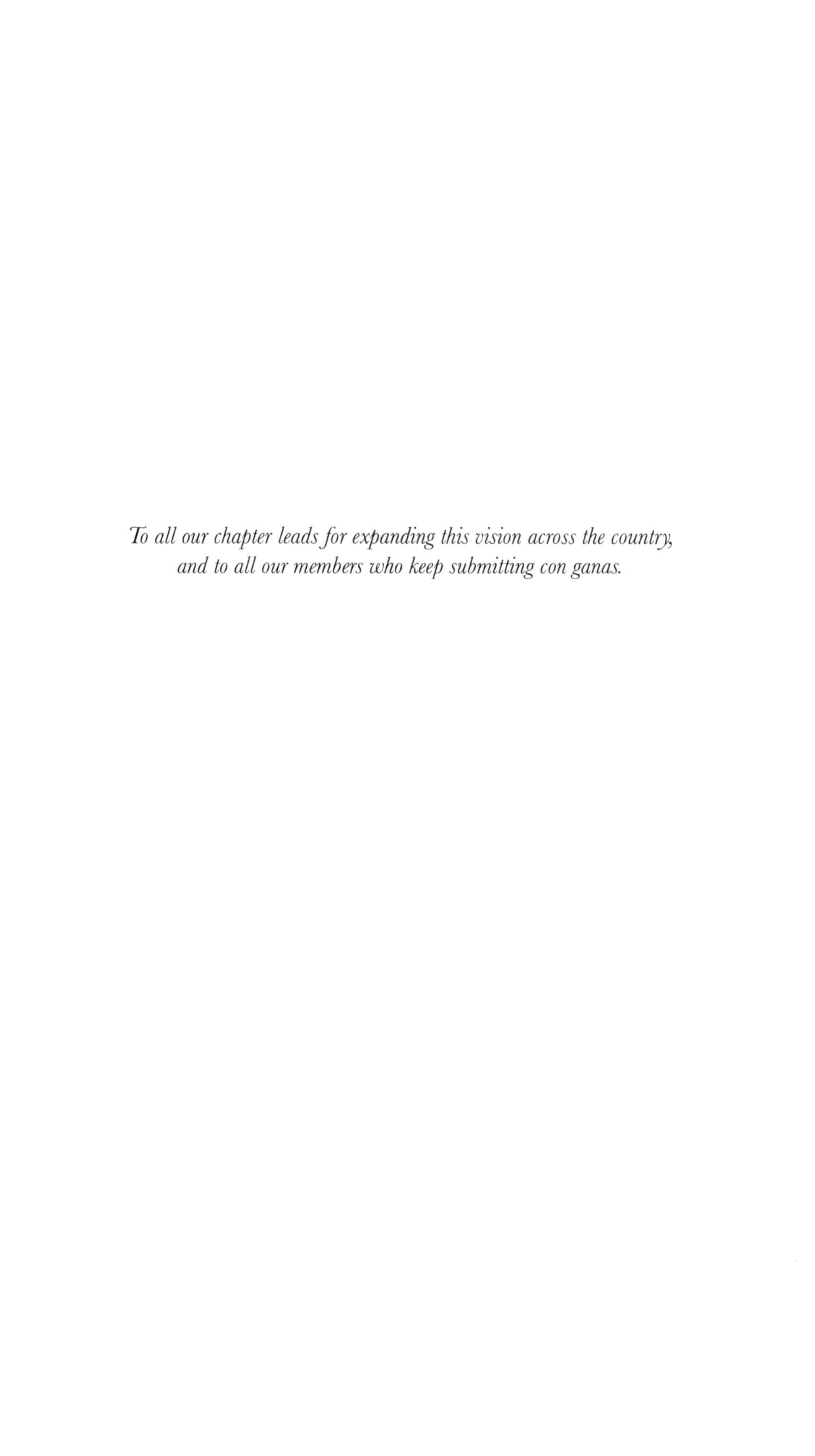

To all our chapter leads for expanding this vision across the country,
and to all our members who keep submitting con ganas.

ACKNOWLEDGEMENTS

This anthology was made possible by the Investing in Tomorrow Organizational Grant from the Center for Cultural Innovation, with support from the William and Flora Hewlett Foundation.

This publication would not be possible without the collaboration of Nikia Chaney at Jamii Publishing.

Muchos thank yous to Sarah Rafael García for her support in the planning process.

Women Who Submit was created in response to the 2010 VIDA Count. We are grateful to VIDA: Women in Literary Arts for their inspiration and commitment to creating transparency around the lack of gender parity in the literary landscape and to amplifying historically-marginalized voices, including people of color; writers with disabilities; and queer, trans and gender nonconforming individuals. (www.vidaweb.org)

CONTENTS

FICTION

NONFICTION

POETRY

FOREWORD

A Legacy of Literary Citizenship

by ALYSS DIXSON, ASHAKI JACKSON, & XOCHITL-JULISA BERMEJO

FOUNDERS OF WOMEN WHO SUBMIT

In 2011, Alyss Dixson, Ashaki Jackson, and Xochitl-Julisa Bermejo established Women Who Submit (WWS) and the submission party concept as a tool for gender parity in publishing. It was an action inspired by the VIDA Count.

WWS is now a literary organization with over 200 local members and 23 chapters across the nation. Its eight-person leadership team collaboratively organizes bi-monthly public workshops, an online community, literary events, fundraising, and the gifting of $1,500 annually in individual grants to empower women and non-binary writers to submit work for publication and build meaningful literary careers.

Much has changed over the years. For one, Alyss has moved from Los Angeles to pursue art and academic opportunities. Yet, the three co-founders reconvened to discuss the organization's beginnings, the anthology's meaning to WWS, and its importance to the literary landscape they sought to change.

The Submission Party

Alyss Dixson: I think of myself as a seed-planter. I'm not the type to work on a single project for years and years. I admire people who are like that, and I try to seek them out. I met Ashaki at a co-working space in Santa Monica and immediately loved her energy. She is a dynamic, funny, brilliant person. An amazing poet. Definitely one of the most encouraging people I've ever met. I was also working with a Black women writers group called the Finish Party. We'd meet every few months to review our manuscripts and encourage one another, fellowship, eat, talk story. It was probably one of the most empowering creative gatherings I'd ever been a part of, and when I began working with WILA: Women in Literary Arts (which later became VIDA), I became more convinced that professional women working together in a way that honored our different communication styles, not replicating patriarchal structures, could be powerful. And then the following spring VIDA came out with our first multi-outlet count.

Ashaki M. Jackson: VIDA's goal was to count the women in select top tier publications (big readership, pay for authors, stamina in the business, etc.). The count was designed as quality assurance—a strategy to make sure women were represented. Little did we know how scant representation was. VIDA blew the industry's cover, so to speak. The impetus to find a solution felt dire.

AD: I'd written a response piece to The Count and been part of the conversations about the various Op-Eds resulting from it. It seemed to me that an important part of repairing this publication problem was not just upping women's submissions, but thinking about the social and structural dynamics that prevented or hindered women from submitting.

AJ: Alyss is practical. She can be a rabble-rouser, and she knows where to best direct her energy to affect change. When we discussed The Count's outcomes, she proposed women assemble solely to submit. There were already so many generative writing groups and workshops. Where was the dedicated space and time to disseminate the writing? To Alyss and me—who were both mid-manuscript at the time—our absence from these publications was an active blockade. We knew too many women writers personally for publications to lack women among their pages. Editors seemed steadfast in attributing our absence from publications to us. We were either too fearful to submit, according to them, or we were submitting things that people (e.g., male editors) didn't want to read. The conversation was low on accountability. We knew there was a need to take stock of women's engagement with the submission process.

AD: We hadn't explored the psycho-social aspects of how submission works. How did women handle rejection? How could we create a dynamic that supported and empowered the kind of growth you need as a writing professional to continue to submit, to take those rejections and turn them into fodder for the next submission? How could we create an atmosphere that was resource rich and encouraged participants to think of research and reading as part of their professional development, not just a necessary evil?

AJ: The submission party was an effort to balance the big lean into space reserved for male authors. We wanted the party to be a closed, exclusive space wherein women could discuss their fears and hesitations around submitting work, engaging editors, identifying fitting publications. The space would be far from the male gaze and that brand of commentary that weighs down academic and community workshops. It would be a space where we delivered our writing and ourselves to editorial teams around the globe in search of acceptance. It would be a soft landing for any rejections, and it would be a stern champion of resubmission. The submission party would be a brain trust. Honestly, we didn't know the shape of the party while thinking of its greatness, but we knew how we needed it to function.

AD: Ashaki introduced me to Xochitl and we strategized a format that could address these concerns (and more, no doubt).

Xochitl-Julisa Bermejo: My focus was creating a warm and welcoming space for writers. The first submission party was in my parents' home, so I felt a personal obligation. In our planning, we established a collective culture by emphasizing the importance of sharing food, journals, resources, and industry insight, or what we lovingly call chisme, at each gathering. In recent years, I've come to understand how this collective culture, which includes the idea that each person at the table is a resource, is the crux of our fight against capitalism and patriarchy, but in the beginning it was simply, how can I help each writer feel supported?

An Exclusive Space

AD: I work as an educator and read a lot in the field. Around the time I decided to start working with VIDA, I'd become invested in how we address equality issues, not just equity issues. With equality we each get a $1, regardless of the circumstances that we bring to the table, that we face outside of the room, our internal strengths or challenges. Equity, on the other hand, concerns itself with removing structural and social barriers. So, maybe Mx. X needs $40, and Mx. Y only needs 0.50. Or maybe no one actually needs any money and a collaboration is the best way to move forward.

Very early on, we predicated WWS on the principle that women, non-binary people, and transgender people, have our own ways of being and doing. We wanted to create a place that builds capacity in participants and remakes submission culture instead of having it be this constant tallying of who got in where, who had how much published this year, etc. To my mind, those are the products of a toxic patriarchal culture and I reject that that is the only way to be in the world. Outright reject it.

XJB: Someone might look at this anthology and question how we can reject these structures and at the same time celebrate these publications, but a wide world of work exists behind each publication that many readers will never see.

A comment I often hear from members is how much they love our monthly rejection brag—a discussion on our closed online forum where members can share the various places that rejected them each month (a concept taken from another closed feminist writing forum). I mean, to celebrate "failure" is a direct affront to patriarchal beliefs.

AD: It's beautiful watching WWS unfold and seeing this vibrant culture of creation and support. Writers are growing into professional careers, some already in professional careers are sharing and mentoring, others who were perhaps burnt out are submitting again. Yes, we track numbers and applaud and commiserate over the publications. But, and this is a big deal to me, the WWS culture is such that we recognize those numbers as a by-product of writing and submitting the work. It's not the work, and it in no way reflects on the writer's worth.

Naming Ourselves

AJ: There is no remarkable origin story behind the name. We aimed to avoid the male gaze by creating an exclusive space, yet our title became a controversial distraction because the male gaze is invasive and can be carried—with intention—by persons who aren't male. Alyss and I wanted to name what we do [submit], then do the work.

AD: For me, the concept of submission is very much tied in with Buddhism. So, this Western notion that submission is a pejorative thing, a thing that happens to you, rather than something you are actively doing, honestly, did not occur to me until I heard feedback.

AJ: Persons unfamiliar with the community and even those new to the community brought questions and accusations of purposeful innuendo. They suggested that the name didn't hold our mission's fully progressive, feminist aspirations. It did to us, and it still does. Yes, we are aware that being submissive carries the weight of women's oppression. Consider this: submit also means to turn in the work you've been hiding in your top drawer. Let's entertain that definition because, as writers, we have broader vocabulary than the average non-reader; because we hold the terms that are truest to our struggle; and because it's OK—even encouraged—to put down/leave behind that gaze.

AD: I find the double entendre of "submit" a motivator. One one hand it is an active process of putting work up for inclusion in a publication and, on the other, it is a process of acceptance and humility, the recognition that you are part of a larger world and not in control of anything but your own actions. When you accept that, you are accepting yourself and that certainly makes one bolder and fearless. I'd like to think of these submission parties as building character in the participants, giving space to vent and process our fears and allowing us to dare to dream with one another. Who doesn't love a party every time you hit the SUBMIT button on a piece you've spent months, maybe years, of your life on?

Documenting the Gains

XJB: When I was invited to help with the creation of the first submission party, I had not yet heard of VIDA and their count of top journals, but learned from what Alyss and Ashaki shared with me in early planning meetings. What stood out was the common narrative from editors that women don't submit as often or resubmit as aggressively as men, which is why women's presence is low. It puts the fault on women writers instead of long-standing patriarchal models that have never asked for or nurtured women's and other marginalized people's voices. When I read this collection, I'm filled with joy to see how untrue this narrative can be. All the writers in this anthology (as well as countless not in these pages) are champions of their work despite the various barriers they face from an industry, country, and society that never wanted them to succeed.

The work in this anthology is necessary, questioning, and honest. Writers respond to police violence and racist political agendas; tease out questions of identity; reflect on motherhood and the importance of women relationships; and knit joyous and fanciful stories. It is what I've always hoped would come from fighting for gender parity in publishing, which is a brighter and more complex literary landscape that pushes the collective understanding of humanity.

A Legacy for the Literary Landscape

AJ: We always want to be in conversation with the intent behind The Count, meaning that we want members to increase their submission output to reduce the disparity in representation. As part of that work, we also want members to extend their submission—to leverage the skills they develop during submission parties and apply this muscle to residencies, workshops, grants, academic opportunities, editorial roles. Further, the submission party is an incubator for literary citizenship. Over time WWS members have inserted themselves more fully into the literary landscape in ways that create pathways for writing by women, non-binary writers, and transgender writers.

INTRODUCTION

Submission as Social Action

by XOCHITL-JULISA BERMEJO

from *LUNCH TICKET*

Once when I was in my early 20s, the tires on my car had gone bald, and my mother offered to take me to Sears to get replacements. At the time I didn't even know the department store sold tires. And who still shopped there anyway? But my mom assured me that with a Sears credit card we could get a good discounted price. Having been a working mother of four for over 30 years, she knew more about this than me, and being a new teacher with few funds, I happily accepted her help.

"Will you be paying with a Sears card today, ma'am?" a boyish, blond cashier asked. My car sat on new tires just outside the automatic doors, keys in the ignition.

"I lost the card, but I can give you my ID." My mother tugged at her license stuck in a bulging wallet the shape of a brick and handed over an ID that displayed the same address she lived at since 1974. I wasn't born until 1980, but 1974 is an important date in my family's history because it is the year my parents moved from an apartment in Boyle Heights, a low-income neighborhood in East L.A., to their first and only house in San Gabriel, a sunny suburb 10 miles east of Downtown Los Angeles nestled below the San Gabriel Mountains. At the time, my oldest brother was only three and my mother was 8 months pregnant with my second brother.

"I'm sorry, ma'am, but your name isn't on this card," the cashier said.

"That's my husband's name," my mother said with a flick of her hand. My cheeks flushed because she never had patience for cashiers, phone tellers, or repairmen.

"But it's not your name, ma'am, so I can't take it," the cashier said looking nervous.

"Well, I wasn't allowed to have a credit card when we got it," she said matter-of-factly, and the skinny, reed of a cashier with loose blond hair and I shared puzzled looks.

"Mom, what do you mean you weren't allowed to have a credit card?" I asked confused.

"It's an old card," she sighed, "I never come to Sears. I don't know, maybe I won't come back." She snatched her ID from the cashier and stuffed it back into her wallet, and stuffed the wallet back into her over-filled purse that sat sprawled and gaping over the counter like a sinkhole.

"I'm sorry ma'am," he said hurriedly going back to the keys of the cash register, "I guess I can do it this once." Within minutes the transaction was finished, and we were walking out sliding glass doors to my newly re-tired car.

It was a sunny afternoon. The San Gabriel Mountains created an impenetrable wall behind the parking lot that mirrored the walls I now imagined around my mother, walls I had never before considered.

"Mom, you couldn't have a credit card?" I asked still dumbfounded.

"No. Back when we first got it, they would only let men have credit cards. I had to put it under your father's name." We climbed into the car.

"You put it under dad's name?"

"Well, yeah. I applied for the card, but I couldn't use my name. I had to use his." She was short in her answers, and maybe still agitated by the cashier, so I silenced my questions, started the engine, and drove us home, just two women fixing a car.

Until that moment, I had never realized how close I was to a completely different reality from the one I lived. I was just one small generation away from living in a society that did not allow women to have credit cards, which meant they couldn't buy their own cars or own property.

The car my mother helped me with was an army green 2004 Scion xB. It was my very first new car, and I bought it with a $2000 down payment I saved from my first year of teaching high school English at a tiny private school in Arcadia. Like the car, the full-time job was a first too. When it came time to sign a loan, my mother agreed to cosign.

I remember sitting side by side at the banker's desk, the contract lying out in front of us.

"Why are these numbers different?" I pointed to two places where the monthly payment did not match.

"The payments are scheduled for the fifteenth of the month, but today is the eighth. If we schedule payments for the eighth of the month, it won't be different. Do you want that?" he asked me.

"Yes, let's do that," I said. After he made the adjustment, I signed, my mother signed, and then he took us out to the lot to show me my new car.

"You made me so proud, mija," she said when we met back at home.

"How?" I asked.

"The way you looked over the numbers and asked questions. That made me very proud." I never thought I was any different from her, but looking back now, I see it's possible.

In 2011, I co-founded an organization with two other women called Women Who Submit. Our focus was to empower women writers to submit work for publication after VIDA: Women in Literary Arts began counting how many women were published in top literary journals. What they found was no surprise, compared to men women were grossly underrepresented in the highest most prestigious literary journals. When VIDA started asking editors why the numbers were so, the most common reply was, "women don't submit as often men." And many believed that statement because women are believed to be quieter than men, less aggressive, and yes, submissive.

When I think of submission and women, I never think of my mother. I think of grandmothers. I think of the 1950s kitchen. I think of a poster I once saw of a woman in a nothing but an apron holding a beer next to a banner encouraging, "Know how to keep your man happy." And even though my mother was born in 1947, I never thought of her living in that time. Maybe it is because my mother has never been the submissive type. In fact, she despises submissive women with their soft giggles and simple-minded pretenses. I was taught at an early age that I was just as strong and just as smart as boys, and I could never act otherwise. If my three older brothers could do it, so could I. Baseball, camping, 20-mile bike rides to the beach, algebra summer school classes, if it was good enough for her boys, it was good enough for her girl.

In her own life, my mother worked full-time in Downtown L.A. offices as secretaries and clerks, but also took the jobs no one else wanted like the office emergency manager—this person created the office emergency plans and scheduled earthquake drills. I never saw her do this job, but I imagine her wearing a hardhat and barking orders. At home, it was often my brothers' and my responsibilities to put dinner on the table and keep the house clean. This makes it sound like my father was not there, but he was. While my mother worked full-time and we were expected to keep the house, my father was allowed to follow his economic dreams and whims after he lost his job as a welder. There was a video rental store, a flower shop, a burrito stand, a party balloon business, a catering business, and weekends spent selling cowboy boots, serapes, and whatever goods my father could pick up on turnarounds to Tijuana at charradas and banda concerts at the Pico Rivera Sports Arena. My mother worked Monday through Friday keeping the steady money coming in, but come Saturday she rose early to cook a vat of beans for burritos or drove to the flower shop in East L.A. to bunch batches of white roses into prom corsages and boutonnieres. This was my first introduction to women's work and gender roles, and from what I saw women could do anything because my mother did everything.

Women Who Submit was created with the idea that if we hosted submission parties—meet ups for women writers in private homes where women could ask questions, gain support and resources, set goals, and submit work in real time—maybe more women would submit regularly and maybe the numbers would change. Think of a women's 1950s Tupperware party, but instead of sharing products to improve our kitchens we shared information to improve our chances of being published in the literary journals of our choosing.

Our first submission party was in July 2011 in my mother's house in San Gabriel. Six women gathered around my mother's kitchen table to create a lending library of literary journals, share food and drink, establish personal goals and submit work for publication. Every time a woman pressed "send" we cheered and clapped. And this is how the first submission party was born.

Soon after, we started to think of a name. I suggested "Ladies who Submit" because it reminded me of "Ladies who Lunch" and thought it was a fun play on an activity seen as benign and shallow. But that got vetoed for Women Who Submit. I didn't think much of the name at the time or the double entendre until other women began to hear of us and make comments.

"Do you know what comes up when you Google Women Who Submit?" one woman prompted. When I tried, I found Bible verses, Christian sites, and the headline, "Submit to your Husband: Should Women be Submissive?"

Recently, our Facebook page received a message from a woman who was recommended to our site by a friend. She wrote: "I have to say, I was thrown by the name of the group. I lived through the '50s...Cool idea...scary name."

This statement made me realize that Women Who Submit is in fact the perfect name for our organization because at its core it is a social action that helps women break free of societal boundaries caused by centuries of female submission.

Sometimes I think $0.77 to every dollar a man makes isn't so bad. Sometimes I think 20% less representation in journal A isn't so bad when journal B has equal representation. But then I think of my mother and how unbearably close it was that women couldn't apply for credit cards, or own property, or work in an office without being harassed. The Clarence Thomas case took place in 1991, and it was only a short 24 years ago that the name Anita Hill and the term "sexual harassment" came into our public consciousness. And then I think of Juarez, Mexico where in the present day women are abducted and killed while on their way to work. And I think of those young women in Nigeria who were kidnapped from their beds and sold off because they wanted to go to school. And I think of women in Saudi Arabia being threatened with imprisonment and violence if they dare to drive.

Women Who Submit is a group of women who submit work for publication because they refuse to be marginalized. Through the support of community and resources we seek empowerment and equality in our chosen professions as writers, editors, and publishers. But more than that, it represents a voice for all women who refuse to be intimidated or silenced.

When I think of my mother, I think of her hard edges, her refusal to accept "no" and her ability to put her head down and do the dirty work. She's a bulldozer, and I think maybe she got that way because no one else fought for her. No one else cheered her on. No one ever told her, "You made me so proud."

Mom, you make me *so* proud!

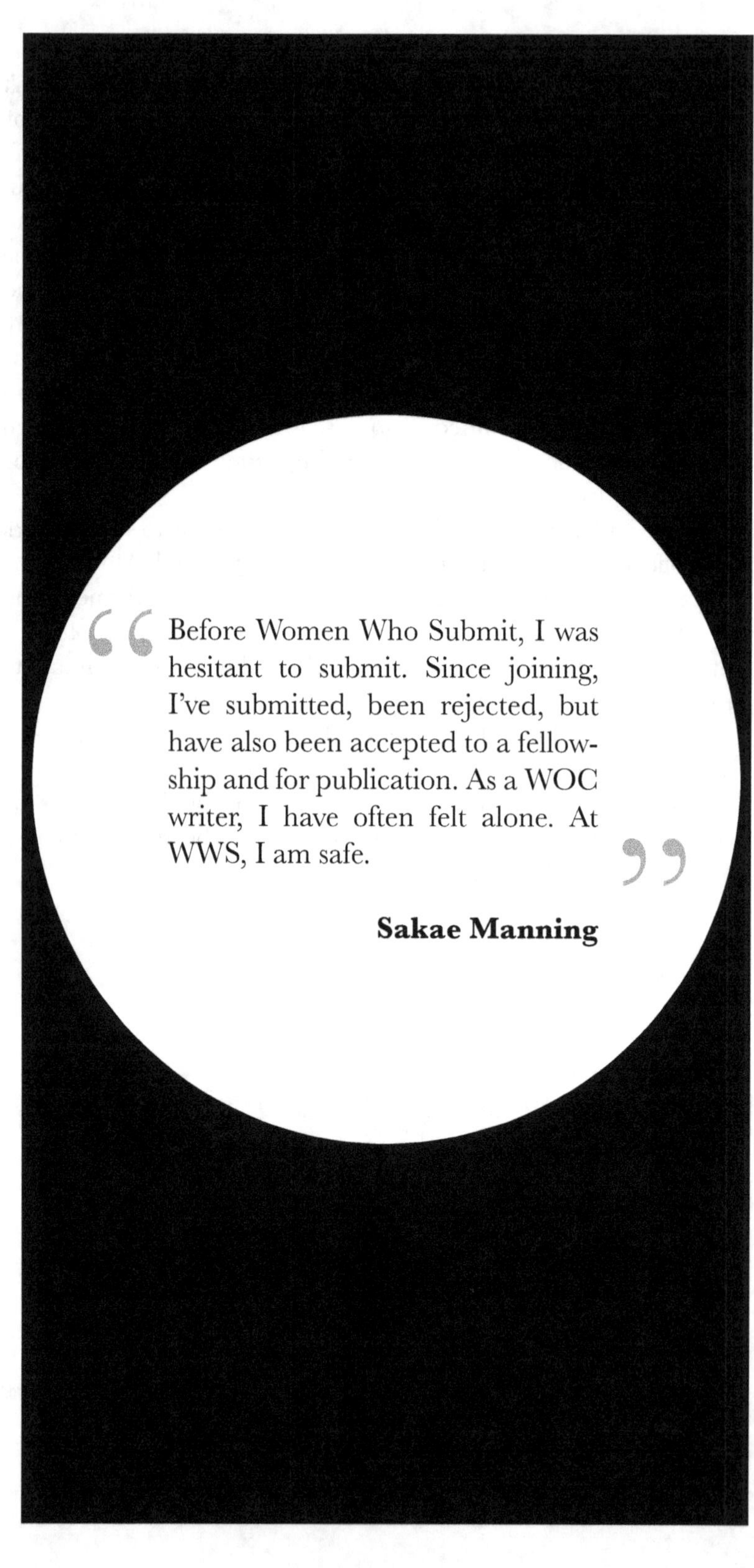
“Before Women Who Submit, I was hesitant to submit. Since joining, I've submitted, been rejected, but have also been accepted to a fellowship and for publication. As a WOC writer, I have often felt alone. At WWS, I am safe.”
Sakae Manning

'I am broken by the revolt exploding inside me'

by MINAL HAJRATWALA

from *RESISTING ARREST: POEMS TO STRETCH THE SKY*

'I am broken by the revolt exploding inside me'

—*Namdeo Dhasal*

Your rage is pomegranates spilling open on ice, is the flute's silver seam, is a volcano spitting rivulets of fire to wash clean these corrupt lands. Your rage is solidarity before after & during the hashtag. Your rage is the angel of karma before after & during the video. Your rage throbs tight in your chest against symbologies of sticks & stones & chokes that break ligament & bone. Your rage is the fulcrum of your desire, chimaerae busting out of cages, heart-sparks flying. Your rage gets shit done & it is no joke. Your rage is the luminous gold truth of sunrise, what you sit with long enough to dissolve your fear. Your rage is a checkmate to your compromise. Your rage is heat from a magnifying glass, focused, bursting into flame. Your rage is a cool blue spotlight circling the empty stage. Your rage is the dog who won't lie down for the wrong master, fierce hen who won't be moved till her brood is hatched, moth who unbinds her cocoon & lifts her body toward light. Your rage is a lesson & you learn it as you breathe. Your rage is this holy sword slicing through stone walls. Your rage is a sentence that says what it must, full-stop. Your rage is our dream of a sweeter brighter world. Your rage is this oar treading the sea to steer this ship this gorgeous fucking hot mess goddamn revolution.

Officer of the Year

by MINAL HAJRATWALA

from *FEMINIST FORMATIONS: POESIA*

I need the whole story before I can say a child is being hurt. I need the whole story before I can say you hurt her. I need the whole story before I can say she hurts. I need the whole story before her hurt is real to me. I need the whole story before I can say she is a child. I need the whole story before I can say she is my child our child somebody's child. I need the whole story before I can say he hurt her in a place where a person hurts if you hurt them. I need the whole story before I can say he threw her to the ground. I need the whole story before I can say he put his knees into her back to hold her down. I need the whole story before I can say how green the grass was underneath where he hurt her. I need the whole story before I can say she was barefoot in a swimsuit & he was uniformed, bootshined, armed. I need the whole story before I can say her swimsuit was the color of a country on fire. I need the whole story before I can say he pulled a gun. I need the whole story before I can say the gun was loaded. I need the whole story before I can say guns kill people & people kill people & police kill people. I need the whole story before I can say the white children stood on the other side of the street where the grass was the same green. I need the whole story before I can hear him say, "Sit your asses down!" I need the whole story before I can hear him say it only to the Black boys. I need the whole story before I can hear the Black boys say, "Sir please sir." I need the whole story before I can see him tell the Black girls to walk away from the sitting-their-asses-down Black boys. I need the whole story before I can see the fathers stand around on the sidewalk. I need the whole story before I can say the boy with the camera is white. I need the whole story before I can say what judicious means & force. I need the whole story before I can say this is my country your country our country his country her country. I need the whole story before I can say the pool that stayed empty of Black people that day was blue.

Hair

by ANITA GILL

from *THE IOWA REVIEW*

In 1990, at the age of six, I sat on the edge of my mother's bed and howled in pain while she brushed my thick black curls with the futile hope of making my hair tame and presentable. Her shoulder-length light brown hair was perfectly set on her head thanks to half a can of hairspray she applied each morning, the scent burning my nostrils as I suffered nerve damage to my scalp. My mother worked the brush from the top of my head down to my split ends. She took sections of my hair in one hand and brushed, her fair-skinned hands disappearing in my long tendrils. I saw my mother's reflection in the closet mirror, her mouth slightly open, her brows furrowed, a face that expressed surprise and wonderment at the mane she tried to beat down, astonished this kid was biologically hers.

My hair color and thickness came from my father. In his expired Indian identification papers, his long black hair was wrapped in a bun just north of his forehead. The red cloth of the Sikh turban covered the bun. His current driver's license displayed black hair cut short and gelled back with a side part. He combed it in the mornings post-shower while a small silver radio blasted tinny songs in Hindi on his bathroom counter.

On this morning, my father was absent from the house, already making rounds at the hospital. Anxious to be outdoors, I squirmed under my mother's hands. "Hold still," she said, and she pressed her fingers to my temple to make me face one direction. Ignoring my whimpering, she brushed more aggressively in places with the most resistance. "Are you almost done?" I asked. A frustrated sigh blew through her mouth.

A glitter ball hair tie lay on the ripples of the quilt, looking like the number "8" with a large sparkly purple bead on each loop. My mother gathered all of the strands around her thumb and middle finger, and then she pulled the hair tie around the thick trunk now set high on the back of my cranium. The lavender brush on the bed had accumulated a cloud of dark brown hair, the part of me my mother removed from the bristles and threw in the trash.

I let my eight-year-old legs dangle over the leather salon chair seat while I overheard my mother make a request to Antoinette, my stylist and early 90's cultural icon. My mother specifically wanted my hair cut much shorter and therefore easier to brush. Antoinette nodded, her short spiked reddish-brown hair barely moving. She took out my glitter ball tie and pulled front strands over my face.

"Look at this beautiful hair!" Antoinette said as she caught my eye in the mirror and smacked her gum. With ice-blue eyes and dark, dyed locks, her appearance channeled Madonna. Each strand of her gelled hair fell perfectly around her heart-shaped face, edgy, cool, effortless.

On the salon floor, my chopped hair became tumbleweeds rolling away as Antoinette worked a blow dryer and barrel brush through my shoulder-length do. My hair fell silky straight. I touched a small smooth clump, understanding what the girls in my class felt when they absentmindedly ran their fingers through their hair. And bangs! My new hairdo included bangs that flowed down my forehead and stopped at the top of my pastel pink glasses. Each strand came straight down, a curtain over my forehead.

Antoinette unhooked the black styling cape and I inched forward in the salon chair, turning my head and watching my hair fan like I was in a shampoo commercial. Back in the car, I pulled down the visor to make sure my salon hair wasn't an illusion.

The next day though, it was gone. Like Cinderella's magical makeover, my smooth silky hair disappeared after my morning shower. I held a lock and random strands plucked out every which way like broken strings on a violin. And yet, between my mother and me, detangling sessions were less strenuous. I no longer yelped as if a dislocated shoulder was being popped into place.

Not long after the haircut, my mother came into my bedroom with clothes wrapped in clear plastic. She told me to put them on. I tied the buttercup colored drawstring pants around my waist while my mother bunched up the matching-hued tunic. She guided the shirt through my outstretched arms. The fabric felt snug around my chest, a size too small. There was embroidery on the front of the long shirt with embedded small mirrors.

My grandparents from India sat in the living room talking with my father in a foreign language. The clinks of their teacups echoed down the hallway. The clothes came from them, a gift. My mother smoothed out the shirt and its obvious fold lines. I whispered to her that it felt itchy. "Well, you just have to show Beeji and Papaji and then you can change," she said. She then helped my younger sister get into hers, a similar outfit, a salwar kameez. I picked at the cuff of my shirt while I stared with envy at my sister's dress, a deep eggplant. With our mother touching our backs, we were paraded into the living room like we were in special costumes for a theatrical performance. If that were the case, we brought the house down. Once our grandparents saw us, they clapped and beckoned us to their side for hugs and more words with funny vowel sounds. My father translated. They thought we looked beautiful. Mom pulled out her Fujifilm plastic camera, snapped a photo, and then cranked the wheel for the next one. My grandmother wore a similar dress in cotton and not covered in embroidery. Hers felt soft from wear and washes. Once my mother ran out of film in the camera, she brought us back to our room.

"Can I change now?" I whined. I pulled at the collar and tried to get the itchy embroidery off of my skin. "You can get back into your regular clothes," she said. And with that I tore off the "irregular" clothes that came from the other side of the world.

*

In 2001, twelve college application papers covered the mahogany table in our rarely used dining room.

My math teacher once said that clear handwriting displayed the writer's confidence. With a sleek black pen, I filled out the general information with careful loops and dots: name, address, birthdate. At the next section, I came to a full stop, the portion with the title "Race/Ethnicity." The instructions said to check the box that most appropriately describes you. One box, singular, yet upon scanning the list, two options seemed equally feasible: White and Asian/Pacific Islander.

I had seen this question before back in my Catholic elementary school on standardized testing days. Before we started the test, we completed personal information and learned how our individual identities were nothing more than a conglomeration of filled bubbles on paper. The categories were the same as these college applications, one box for White, one for Asian/Pacific Islander. The instructions on the tests said to check one. As a nervous elementary school student, I pulled at a piece of my shoulder-length hair and twirled it between my index finger and thumb. I didn't dare raise my hand and ask my white teacher or any of the white students in my class. I had enough anxiety about standing out amongst my peers because they all knew one of my parents didn't attend church and wasn't even Christian. While staring at the box, I agonized that I'd mark it incorrectly and incite an investigation hearing, a lamp shining in my face. Some years I filled in White. Other years, I filled in Asian. Then other years, I filled in Other. And after the teacher scooped up the tests I forgot about my identity marker. No one said anything. No investigators, no bureaucratic pencil pushers set to determine my race fluctuation. This led me to the conclusion: no one cared.

But the university had to be more meticulous, surely. These papers ushered me into the doors of higher ed. Hearing my mother in the kitchen, I called for her help. She appeared in the entranceway, still in her teacher's clothes: a long evergreen skirt that matched the vest over her cream-colored blouse.

I explained my predicament and the options. She put one hand on the doorframe while she listened, her face showing no signs of surprise or reflection. Perhaps she'd already thought about this conundrum before, at a time when I was younger and running away from morning hair brushings. I imagined her at a chalkboard, writing out complex formulas involving letters and Greek symbols and coming to the conclusion she would now share.

"Oh, just put White," she said, like the choice was something to shrug off, a rough estimation where you round up from half. I glanced back down at the boxes and chewed on the inside of my lip. I raised my head to dispute her instruction, but the entranceway was empty.

Under my high school information, I jotted down the small private school my parents had enrolled me in, a preK-12 school in Southern Maryland with a mostly white class demographic. My parents decided it was more academically rigorous than the Catholic school I'd attended since kindergarten. In 7th grade, I walked into a new school hoping the small class sizes meant students would clamor to be friends with the new kid. But middle school meant groups of solidified cliques who shot a dirty look in my direction and returned to their clan to murmur. Not long into my stint, I discovered one classmate referred to me as the "Mexican with zits." Another girl came up to me while we changed in gym asking what tanning bed I went to. When I explained to her that I was Indian, she gasped, asked me what tribe because she had some fraction of Cherokee in her blood.

As these memories replayed in my head, I stared at the list of ethnicities. How could I check the "White" box when white kids constantly pointed out how different I was?

I didn't tell my parents about these incidents. The few times I had confided in them, my parents told me to just ignore other's comments. Neither of them understood what it was like to walk into classrooms looking different from the rest of their peers. To them, the best way to avoid race was to not bring it up. Don't see color. Perhaps in not making it an utterance within our house, the social construct of race would cease to exist in the world. But my parents and I lived in Maryland, the first state in the colonies to have anti-miscegenation laws in the books and one of the last states to finally remove those. Neither of my parents were from Maryland, and yet they raised my sister and me there, a place that allowed interracial marriages only a few years before my parents' wedding. Even with the changed laws, racial mixing was barely visible, and racial groups around me mostly stayed within their categorical perimeters. While my mother's solution for me was to pick the side most visible on my skin, the locals didn't agree.

The sound of oil sizzling in a pan came from the kitchen and brought me out of my memories and back to the application papers. Down the cluster of boxes, I checked "White."

*

I returned home for Thanksgiving during my first semester at college. After getting off the Amtrak train from New York, I found my mother in the kiss-and-ride section of the New Carrolton station parking lot.

Rubbing her gloved hands in the car, she looked up, and when she recognized me and the oblong suitcase I dragged, she jumped out of the car for a hug. "What's going on with your hair?" she asked. In my first semester in college, I had a low-maintenance hair routine down, applying a dollop of electric blue gel into my just-showered hair, which hardened into a crusty crown on top and flowed into corkscrew curls by my shoulders. "Mom, let it go," I said and rolled my eyes.

As we careened down Route 301, my mother talked and occasionally reached for the gear shift. Though we spoke on the phone weekly, my mother had hidden away some stories she decided were better relayed in person. So she did.

At my mother's job at an all-girls Catholic high school, a black student had accused her of discrimination. My mother gave more context, that the girl was a moody freshman in her homeroom that complained constantly. Being that this girl was a pill, my mother dealt with her in the same fashion she would with her own daughters—she ignored her. The student, seeing that my mother wouldn't give her the time of day, believed she was the victim of prejudice.

I stared at my mother's profile in the car while she narrated the story. When I had visited the school in eighth grade, I witnessed the tumult of students opening and closing lockers, chatting, laughing in the brick-lined hallways, a diverse student population where the majority were black, followed by white, and then a smattering of other ethnicities, all donning gray plaid skirts and burgundy polo shirts with the high school crest on the corner. These students took U.S. History with my mother, her classroom decorated with the chronological order of the presidents along with posters of the founding fathers. Outlining our nation's long-standing racist laws was an integral part of her class objectives.

I tried to get out words but felt choked. My mother kept her hands on the steering wheel, looking out the windshield, occasionally shifting gears after passing a bend in the road. "So, what happened?" I asked. She flicked her wrist that it was nonsense. The administration set up a meeting with her, the accused student, and the student's mother. The administration found no wrongdoing from my mother and closed the appeal.

I nodded, the tightness in my chest diminished. Out the window, lone farmhouses and corn fields passed by. Our car sped past the forest of trees, leaves all gone, a dense forest of skeletons. My mother continued reflecting on the whole thing: the meeting, the investigation, the offended party. "She felt I was racist, and I thought 'Really? The woman who is married to an Indian is racist?'"

I mumbled in agreement. The flaws in that axiom would come to me only later, piece by piece, when I finally understood racism to be like a spot on the floor people covered up with a rug. In the car, I was more awash in relief her trouble was over. I didn't stop to think how my mother's defense contradicted how she'd long handled my identity. How could she be married to a nonwhite person and have an all-white kid?

*

In June 2008, when I was twenty-four, I sat on a stiff bed next to my mother, sorting through photographs. An old motorcycle drove by the house, loud and in need of a tune up.

Normally, I didn't opt for cleaning or organizational tasks, but we were in India, my father in the other room talking to my grandmother in the language I'd never bothered to learn, not that anyone in my family had encouraged me to do so. My mother, sister, and I pulled out the piles of dusty photographs from the shelved cabinet in the guest bedroom and figured out which ones were worth keeping. The blurry ones went into the trash pile. The rest were put aside.

I fidgeted and looked around the room for something else to do. My book sat on the side table. I wanted nothing more than to recline on the bed and read while my mother and sister occupied themselves with this pointless categorization, supposedly meant to help my grandmother clean out her closets.

My mother brought a photo to my face. "Look at this," she said. It was a group shot of people in a banquet hall the color of a sunset, taken during my first trip to India at age ten. The celebration was the fiftieth birthday party for my uncle held in an event space at the foot of the Himalayas. My uncle and his immediate family stood in the center, followed by the deluge of relatives, us included. Holding the photo, my mother's index finger hovered over the image of her face. Her hair a frizzy halo because her curling iron melted two days into that trip. "You know, I never considered Indians to be a different race," she said.

For the past few years, my racial identity had been an ongoing argument. As I progressed through college and graduate school with a better understanding of being mixed, my mother would shut me down, telling me Indians were considered white, and therefore I was white. After every confrontation, I left with a sense of emptiness. She was my mother, and without her approval, I couldn't stand on my own. She was an intelligent woman and an educator. And while I didn't totally believe her assertions, what I dreaded most was identifying as mixed and then learning I was mistaken. Nothing frightened me more than being seen as a disillusioned girl desperately adopting a race for attention.

But as the window unit air-conditioner hummed in the house, my mother gave a start at seeing her white complexion stick out among the sea of brown faces. "I guess this means you are biracial," she said. I shrugged and threw more photos down in the pile.

What should have felt like a satisfying redemption of my identity rang hollow. I visited the country where my father lived until he was thirty, and instead of exploring, I isolated myself in the house and watched American DVDs. I was ashamed. I didn't feel Indian. Every night, I happily got into bed, relieved another day ended, and that I was closer to departing. My biracial identity never felt like bridging two worlds—more accurately, it was divisive, forcing me to choose a side.

*

A mound of exam book essays sat on the futon next to me—the physical manifestation of my weekend plans. A headache formed at the bridge of my nose. In 2014, I had acclimated to a position as an adjunct professor at a community college in Southern California. "Like mother, like daughter," people said to me. But I hadn't gone into the profession thinking I wanted to follow in my mother's career path. Still, I pulled out my cell phone and contacted her, telling myself it would be a conversation about pedagogy and therefore a form of professional development rather than procrastination.

Without saying "hello," I vented about my college students and their poor performance, how my carefully constructed lessons weren't sinking in. My mother and I compared notes and cracked jokes, which dissolved my anger. We conversed as adults, as equals. But while talking, I referred to myself as a woman of color and the tone shifted again—she asserted herself as my all-knowing mother and I regressed into the disciplined child.

"Don't say that," she said.

"Why can't I say that?" I asked.

"Because a person of color means something else," she said.

"What does it mean?" I asked.

"Well," she paused. "A person of color is…colorful," she said.

I laughed. The holes in her arguments became clear to me. I stood in her blind spot. Checkmate in three moves. "What does that even mean?" I asked. She struggled to respond. "I don't think about race because it never affected me," she said. I thought to myself, But couldn't you sympathize with the fact that it affected me?

I got off the phone with her feeling agitated. Though I was thirty, she could still make me feel like the seventeen year old among the mess of college applications.

There lay something maternal in her denial of my racial identity, a need to stake her claim on me. She'd told me that race hadn't entered her thoughts when she married my father. But I wonder, when she held me for the first time and saw the mess of black hair covering my scalp, hair that looked nothing like hers, if she realized the journey ahead, the day-to-day chore of proving I was hers. Perhaps there was a protective instinct about her that subconsciously hoped she could convince me to "be white" and therefore obtain the privileges that went with it. Whatever it was, we had far from resolved things. And much like when I'd come home despondent that my students didn't understand the lesson, I hunkered down and reassessed.

The next holiday rolled around and I flew to my mother's. We found each other in the airport and she sang my name as she pulled me into an embrace. As she released me from the hug, she tugged at one of my locks. Her fingers released, and the strands sprung back into a corkscrew curl. "I love what you've done to your hair," she said.

Chamomile Hair

by CYBELE GARCIA KOHEL

from *THESE FRAGILE LILACS POETRY MAGAZINE*

when I was a child my
mother poured cool
chamomile tea in my
hair saying it would
make it soft and
beautiful

at my school reunion one friend
said he didn't recognize me my
blonde locks long retired I didn't
know how to explain it was never
really my color it was my
mother's way of saying she
wished I was something other

Deciduous

by JAMIE ASAYE FITZGERALD

from *THE AMERICAN POETRY REVIEW*

That fall after the baby was born
my hair fell out,

not like antlers or teeth,
but dark streams of worry
down my arms.

The scrawny city tree
in the sidewalk
next to Carl's Jr.—

I caught sight of it
just as a wind
whirled its leaves away.

This is the new you,
ready for winter and risk—

branches that flower
or break.

The Movement

by SARAH RAFAEL GARCÍA

from *THE ACENTOS REVIEW*

"I don't paint dreams or nightmares, I paint my own reality." —Frida Kahlo

You may not believe my tale but let me tell you anyway.

About six months ago, the change in la Chicana began when she was off to a women's circle to call upon her indigenous ancestors. Well, that's what she mentioned to the cell phone. I hung on the far wall while she stood staring at me with the cell phone pressed to her right ear. When guest acknowledged my presence, she referred to me as "Frida's Self-Portrait from 1940." She used words like, "Chingona," "Feminist Icon," and "the Mexican artist I aspire to be," to describe me to everyone. It was normal for her to stand in the middle of the living room with her back to the prayer candle. She called her La Virgencita. But she contemplated ideas rather than prayers to me. She said I inspired her. *But like a mound of tamales the day after Christmas, I too was taken for granted.*

You know, la Chicana once prayed to La Virgencita first, then turned to me with such convoluted ideas, "Right Frida, we'll show them! It's all about the female power! They can't tell us what to do! I'm free spirited like you Frida! I can have sex with whoever I want."

The girl walked away from both of us pushing her cellphone's buttons. Minutes later there was a knock at the front door. I didn't even get to see if they were man or woman. They both raced across the barren floor, kissing and pulling on each other's clothes, straight into the bedroom—only leaving a bra and shoe, like breadcrumbs on a trail. When they disappeared, I noticed La Virgencita burnt brighter than ever before.

That night, La Virgencita's flame danced to the echoes from the bedpost, high pitched coos filled with such vulgarities only the devil could have invented. *Señorita frrree-spirited*, what does she know about real freedom? The real Frida was revolutionary until the end, she lived with pain as a reminder of her existence and purpose—imagine a metal pole thrust through her innards and she survived! She didn't need such tacky rendezvous to feel alive. She calculated each encounter, stitched each thread of her life into a life-size rebozo hung on the shoulders of every Mexicana who defied any social roles—at least that's what the one prior to la Chicana said aloud during a party she hosted. Yes, the change in la Chicana clearly started the day when I spoke about the duende to La Virgencita.

As soon as la Chicana locked the front door on her way to the women's circle, La Virgencita, who seemed to draw more attention than me because she was a three-dimensional relic, spoke from across the room.

"Oye comadre, tell me one of those passionate stories again."

She couldn't help to call out every time we were alone—particularly when she had no new prayers to handoff to the real Virgin Mary for la Chicana. La Virgencita often asked about the real Frida but on that particular day I wanted to share something different, I wanted to be more than just stories of what I was supposed to represent. But la Virgencita was unrelenting.

"Andale Frida, tell me a story, don't act like you're all innocent. If I can't live through you, then what am I to do? Sit here and talk to these 'made in China' seashells?"

Paper mâché marigolds, seashells, some burnt sage, and smaller candles were placed all around La Virgenicita. From the crooked angle in which I hung, I could see the moon shine in from the single, front window. La Virgencita sat on the second shelf with no real view but of the backside of the futon and me straight-ahead. The double bolted door was on the right and the kitchen I never got to see was on her left. But she always received special offerings from la Chicana. La Virgencita's original wax was halfway burnt. Lucky for her, she always received a new votive candle, placed on top during full moons—it was la Chicana's only routine.

You know, la Chicana found me at the same thrift shop as the bookcase that displayed La Virgencita, over two years ago—but that feisty prayer candle came into la Chicana's life long before I came along. La Chicana once said to a friend, "My mama passed it on to me when I was little girl, to protect me from evil and the duendewho distracted me from cleaning my room,"—that's how she explained it and often went on to say she put all her faith in La Virgencita.

Sometimes La Virgencita was lit with green or red candles but for the most part la Chicana preferred the color white. La Chicana was very spiritual in that way—or so I thought. Sometimes la Chicana offered La Virgencita fresh wild flowers, copal incense and Mexican sweets. I knew the prayer candle must've been verrry especial to have her verrry own shelf on the bookcase, but I would have never thought anything else. But like the saying goes, *water from candy can kill you, and she who takes care of you will make you crawl for the things you want.*

So, I fell for La Virgencita too, and started telling a story, "Bueno ok Virgencita, I'll share a story. But no more of Diego or communist lovers—let me speak of the forgotten myths that in these days never get told by this new generation."

"Forgotten myths? Are you trying to convert me Frida? Ay por favor, I'm just a candle and you're just a replica. Not even a real painting. Don't be trying to talk all-fancy now. Andale cabrona, maybe the one about the sexy jazz singer? You know the dark-skinned woman they say you took to bed one time. Now that's a tale I want hear about again." This time La Virgencita chuckled so hard her flame went out. But as animated as she was, she nonchalantly relit her flame before the smoke cleared. I should've known better, *because where there's smoke, there's always something brewing.* Well, at least that's what la Chicana's mama used to say. But that day, la Virgencita was quite persistent and I was bored with our own ritual.

"Ay Virgencita, they are just stories. Why do you want to hear me tell'em again? You see, I'm always here just like you—except I hang uneven on this eggshell wall. It is you she seeks for comfort. Me? I'm just a colorful icon."

We hadn't been at the apartment verrry long, but after two years of going back and forth between roommates and her mother's home, la Chicana finally got her own place. Si, si, I should've been pleased. After all, I did have my own wall. But I knew it was just a matter of time. She was a painter—a Chicana muralist. But the mujer barely had money to fill her gas tank. Then she got herself this big condo on the eastside walking distance to the park filled with old oak trees, near the river, close to el centro and lots and lots of shops, blah, blah, blah—that's all I heard her say to the cell phone, over and over again.

"Oh mama, you shouldn't worry. It's a nice place, near the lake and a park filled with trees. The condo is near lots of shops, soon I will be able to shop there too. What are you talking about? Mama, duendes don't exist. Why are you so traditional? I'm moving on up mama, isn't that what you wanted for me? Si, of course, I always light my prayer candle."

I too listened like the cell phone. La Chicana came to me with her problems and emotions, but she never offered anything to me. And now look where I am. *Give someone a hand and they give you their foot.*

But La Virgencita finally did let me tell my story, "Fine, so what new cuento do you have for me Frida? Don't start talking about La Llorona or the Boogie man, because I heard all about them already." In that moment her flame grew so tall that the old singed area on the above shelf got twice as wide.

I went along with her request, "Bueno, there are old tales of these mischievous creatures who roam in forests and sometimes near bodies of water. They are known to be short and verrry ugly with long hair. Longer than our hair and they are more like men of course. Verrry ugly. Dwen-des, yes, she called him a duende. I don't know if it's magical, but it is some sort of myth. It is said duendes are known to distract children, take them out to play in the trees or along the water's edge, show them to care more about candy, toys and material stuff like that. You see duendes will give children anything as long as they get attention and bring them the offerings they request like food and whatever else they want. Duendes want to be the center of the child's attention."

"It sounds like the child gets more than the duende, no?"

La Virgencita seemed to be genuinely interested, so I continued.

"But a legend follows them, Mexican parents don't like their children playing with duendes because sometimes their children disappear or are found floating in the rivers and lakes—fooled by all the false promises made by the duende. Actually, if I remember right, they are all over, from the rainforests of Belize to even the rocks and caves of the Philippines."

La Virgencita interrupted, "Ay Frida, you expect me to believe that? Doesn't the Irish leprechaun get his day here, where everyone dances in the streets wearing his color and filled with his spirits? Mira, he even promises a pot of gold and we don't see any gold around here, do we? Por favor, whoever you heard talking about these duendes didn't know anything. Just forget the story. And why do you say they are ugly? How would you know, have you seen one?"

Before I could answer la Chicana barged through the front door with two other young women. Upon throwing her worn backpack on the couch, she shouted, "Ay that girl thinks she can come into our circle after everyone knows she slept with my ex! Seriously, she has slept with all of the men on the eastside!"

The girl wearing a "Brown & Proud" shirt responded, "Ay Susanna, c'mon like you said, he's your ex. Let's remember the movement is bigger than this."

But la Chicana was too angry. I could see by the way she

pulled on chongo. She shouted again, "The movement? This isn't about the cause or the anti-SB1070 walkouts in 2009—this is about her up in my life! She's everywhere, at the protests, the meetings. She was in one of my classes, now even my women's circle. Man, that slut needs to stay out of my way before my fist goes up straight into her face!"

Then the one carrying a stenciled canvas bag spoke sarcastically, "Oh wow, now you want to call her a slut and threaten with violence? C'mon mujer, we are not supposed to oppress our own. And you don't want bad karma on you, especially when you're about to graduate and start your new job as a badass graphic designer! Mira, look at your Frida on the wall, now ask yourself, what would Frida do?"

At that comment, la Chicana pushed her friend on the shoulder and laughed hysterically. She giggled over and straightened me out, I was almost paralleled to the bookcase.

"We'll show them Frida. I am bigger than all of this. And with you at my side, I know I can do it!"

Smirking, they all sprang to the kitchen in unison, that's when I saw La Virgencita's flame lean in the same direction. She flashed a blazing-blue, then suddenly blinked off like a flashlight.

Ay, the real Frida would smoke a cigarillo right about now or maybe even toss back some mescal to ease the disappointment. What do I know—the real Frida could also be an old folktale. All along I thought La Virgencita asked for Frida's stories to praise her and compliment me. But now, I think I was just temporary wall décor, just something to talk about.

After returning from the women's circle, la Chicana did not leave her studio apartment for the days that followed. She wore the same oversized plaid piyamas pants, white-ribbed tank top and messy chongo on the top of her head for three whole days. In the past, she was never one to show off her slender legs or even her black satin hair, not even when she was the only one in the room. Most of the time her hair was braided to one side and she hid her legs in frayed jeans. The only sign of vanity were her embroidered blouses and vivid rebozos.

During the first two days her nose was buried in graphic art books. Other moments she stared seriously at her loteria journal where she had carefully checked off words she had previously written down. Towards nightfall, she wasted many hours sitting on the couch with her laptop covered in washed-out stickers that read, "Xicana Power," "Stop Deportations" and "Feminist *do it* without you."

On the third day, her cellphone disrupted the silence in the late afternoon with a song, "Yeah, we gotta take the power back… Come on, come on." Upon raising it close to her ear the song stopped, and she began yelling obscenities but not like the ones she shouted in the bedroom. Her last word ended with a guttural sigh. La Chicana tossed the cell phone onto the floor. It bounced a couple of times but survived without damage. While stomping towards the kitchen she grew red in the face and pulled her hair down hysterically. She returned choking a wine bottle in her right hand and chanted twice, "Madrecita, dear God, I'm so over this!" Tears rolled down her tense cheeks while she drank directly out of the "damn cheap bottle of wine," as she had yelled a number of times before it was empty. Sometime after midnight, the bottle rolled under the futon when she nearly fell over the coffee table making her way towards the bedroom.

On the fourth morning, she went to la Virgencita, added three mandarins to the altar and whispered something I couldn't hear. She didn't wear her usual huaraches or converse, not even one of her Mexican-like tops. No, no, that day she wore a plain black dress with a sweater. You know, like the white girls wear—si, they call them cardigans. The real Frida wore rebozos every day, not a car-di-gan—her shoulders were always draped with red or turquoise ones. Well at least that's what la Chicana said when she showed off her collection to her friends.

It is true I'm just a replica—we all are, even you. And we just get passed on from one Chicana to the next, each of them used me as a symbol while telling stories of the real Frida to impress whoever they were trying to outdo in Chicana facts like it was some sort of social status. But one of them—about four Chicanas ago—actually took a class on magical realism and she is the one who spoke openly about myths to her lovers. Si, the writer is mi favorita. She was well educated, well read and she too had mixed blood like the real Frida—I can't remember if she was Irish or German but she was more like the real Frida. She was planning to be a Chicano Studies professor, now that has a real purpose, que no? It was she who handed me to La Chicana.

"Here this is for you, this Frida has helped me along the way. I know she's not like a real painting, but she is still the one who reminded me that my own struggles were nothing compared to the real Frida's daily pain and life in the shadows of Diego. And because of her, we as women and artists get to rebel and create on our own magic within reality. Go on take it, put her up in your living room, talk to her, she's quite reassuring."

Well, she gifted me to one of her friends who needed me more, she said. All the others before her were only about the protests, Chicano moratorium and fists in the air, blah, blah, blah—*just mouths full of honey that later changed into greedy hands*. Most of them lost interest once they graduated from the university, received real paychecks and some of them even traded me out for newer prints of Van Gogh, O'Keeffe and Gustav Klimt.

Anyways, on that day, with her new dress and all, la Chicana also wore her hair down and carried a real purse—not a canvas bag or book-bag—a black-leather clutch tucked under her arm. Si, from that day la Chicana changed—but not like the change she referred to as a result of "the movement."

Later that morning, la Virgencita spoke to me for the first time in a week, "Oye comadre, tell me again about those good-looking duendes."

Honestly, I was quite surprised to hear anything from la Virgencita. Most of the time when la Chicana whispered towards the altar, I wouldn't hear from her for another set of days.

"I said they were verrry ugly—not good-looking. And today you are speaking to me after she whispered to you. That's a first."

She quickly replied, "Well, it's only because your story was en-ter-tain-ing. I do have much to consider today. But tell me more about those duendes you mentioned the other day. I thought you said you had a magical story."

"Virgencita, if you don't believe me then why did you ask me about it? Now, you tell me something. What did la Chicana say to you today? She is acting strange, que no? And did you see what she was wearing today? *More American than a hot dog on 4th of July*.

"You know I can't tell you, I have to pass on her requests to the real Virgin Mary. If not, the poor Chicana will never see her prayers come true. You and I have very different roles Fridita. I mean you are colorful y todo. But me, she can't live without me. I've been with her since she was a niña. I will get passed on to her children too. You, well you know. You'll have to wait and see who your next Chicana is going to be." La Virgencita flickered as if she was covering her chuckles with a real hand.

"Aaaay, I thought you were supposed to be holy and nice. Look, I'm just telling you a story I heard. It was even said they ward off duendes with Virgin candles and crosses, so you will always be important in this world Virgencita. No need to insult me."

"Mira, Señora Replica, why don't you stay out of my business and I'll stay out of yours. I mean the only reason I spoke to you was because I have to stare at you all day long. Pues, you are nothiiing. Someone dumped you out like ba-su-ra, yes just like trash! I was just doing you a favor while you pass the time. Tu sabes, before she passes you along."

I had never seen her burn so high, the top shelf started to smolder. Then just like that the flame vanished. The smoke transformed into a shadow on the wall, swirling in the air, creating a tiny rounded figurine. The peculiar image ran wildly, disappearing into the front door. La Virgencita stopped talking to me that day. She never told me why or answered my comments from across my side of the room ever again. But that shadow, that shadow haunted me for weeks.

*

Three months passed, La Chicana came and went. She moved the altar into her bedroom without public explanation and crammed used books in its place. Days later, I saw the chubby shadow once again. It ran against my wall, waddled up to tap my frame and seeped into the corner towards the outside. I could hear la Chicana start her new car that she bragged about to herself when she walked out the door.

I hung more crooked than I ever did before but now I was also left alone.

As the days progressed, I felt the magenta and turmeric hues fade from the flowers on my canvas. My fabric also withered away, resembling old linen. Each day I was gradually perishing. I started to tell stories about the real Frida just to convince myself that I existed.

After losing count of the nights, la Chicana came in with bags and bags. Some labeled "IKEA," "Target," and "Whole Foods." She added a carpet under the coffee table, traded out her red rebozo decorating her futon with a beige, wool blanket and lit candles labeled "velvet cabernet." And just when I thought she was done with the new décor, she unhooked me from the wall. I was left leaning on the futon, discarded like an empty wine bottle. Can you believe she took the time to carefully mark the wall with a pencil then placed a mirror where I once hung? She even walked backwards away from it. Tilting her head to the right, confirming it lined up perfectly with the ceiling. Si, she made sure the mirror was verrry straight.

Upon smiling at her accomplishment, she ran to her bedroom, spoke giddily to herself and returned in a new black dress. This one was the tightest and shortest I'd ever seen. If I read the three digits on the tag correctly that was no "damn cheap" dress either. Tucking in the price tag under her armpit, she approached the mirror, grinned from ear to ear then proceeded to apply cherry red lipstick, making sure to dab a little more here and there. Talking to it like she used to talk to me. She blew herself kisses and was ignorant to everything else.

Just then, the shadow dashed out from the crease on the left where the wood floor met the wall, gray-like little feet leaped up about ten times like it was climbing a peak, and then it buried itself under the mirror. Just then the pewter frame changed into iridescent silver, even reflected la Chicana as a flawless image with long waves of caramel highlights in her shiny now auburn hair. La Chicana asked for the mirrors approval.

"Mirror, mirror on the wall, do I look good and all?"

While turning to the left, she puckered her lips and twirled away towards the futon. She pulled a shoebox out of yet another bag and placed her freshly-done, red toes into golden-studded sandals.

And just when she was about to lean back onto me, she jumped.

"Ay Frida, you scared me! I have to put you away before all the advertising peeps arrive. I'll show everyone. I caaan be one of them."

And that's how I ended up here.

That same night she lit a new votive and placed some candy at the altar, making sure her room remained closed at all times. I only know this because her new leather-bound journal contained the words she spoke aloud and checked off with a pen. She eventually slid me under her bed. All I heard that evening were heavy steps that caused me to tremble, lots of laughter, lots of request for more wine and not one guest spoke Spanish or even mentioned "the movement."

Not one.

They all kept mentioning the "new opening" for an account executive and how she would be perfect—especially because she was "Hispanic and all"—si, that's what they said. The real Frida would have corrected them. Even the writer would have said, "I'm Mexican-American." But not la Chicana, she just laughed in their accent, she just kept asking for their thoughts on the new mirror.

A couple days after her stylish event, she dropped some mismatching silverware, her huaraches and me here in this box—she told the cellphone she needed to donate a few things before brunch with her new boss. For a moment I thought she remembered what her mama often said, *the richest is not who has more, but who needs the least.* Ay, I think she misunderstood that dicho.

And well, here I am staring at you—who looks just like me. I've never seen another Frida this close, but you do have a slight resemblance to all their descriptions. It's like you're my reflection—a rainbow of flowers on your head, cursed with an austere brow and decorated with a rebozo displaying the pride the real Frida carried on her shoulders. She must be real if we both exist. So, tell me, how did we both end up in this box, *staring at our skeletons and biting our tongues?*

"Um yeah, I don't know anything about no Freeda, Verhenseeta or Spanish. I didn't want to interrupt you for the sake of being entertained and all, but the divorcees picked me up during their honeymoon in Cancoon. My only guess is that they both trashed me. Or maybe want some sort of tax credit. But here we are *like pigs in a blanket.*

"But what did you say about that dwen-dy-shadow agiiin? That ther' sounded like a pesky gnome to me. Oh, what the hell. We got time to kill…let me tell you about the gnome that sat on the porch—that porch that was made to match the white picket fence around the house in the suburbs…"

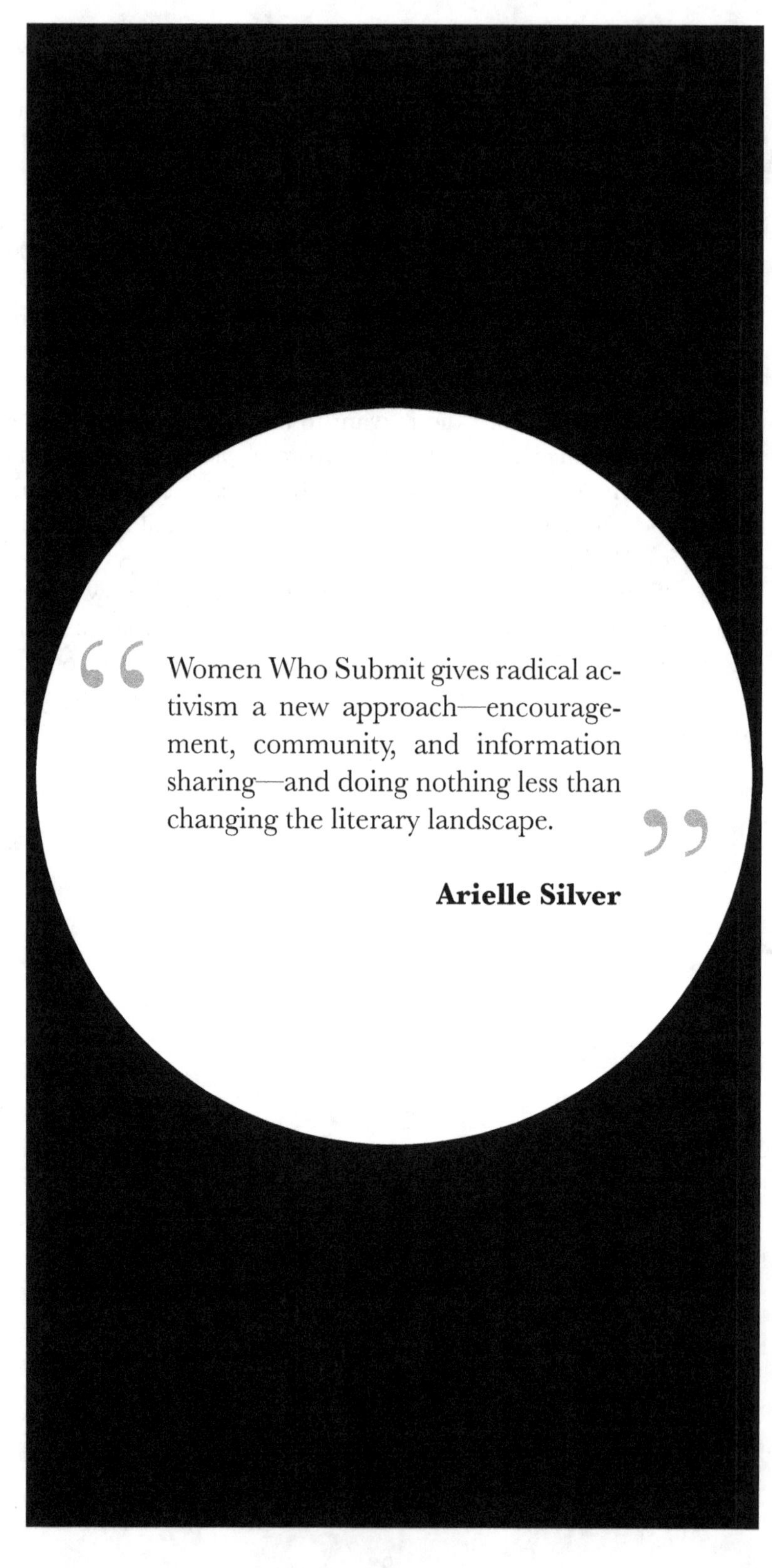
Women Who Submit gives radical activism a new approach—encouragement, community, and information sharing—and doing nothing less than changing the literary landscape.
Arielle Silver

Unbeautiful

by ARUNI WIJESINGHE

from *ALTADENA POETRY REVIEW*

no cornflower-blue eyes
instead burning embers more
suited to kohl than mascara
brows arched in perpetual
surprise

no golden hair that feathers
perfectly à la Farrah Fawcett
repeatedly tucks the same loose
strand behind her right ear

Maybelline ads are wasted
here.

She's not beautiful. self-conscious about
the gap in her front teeth maybe she
smiles anyway

no endless supply of Fair and
Lovely Lightening Cream will
fade cinnamon skin, bark of
some other rare tree

dip of waist flaring
to fecund curves
prized in the
tropics, not here in
this City of Angels

No two-inch thigh gap
here.

speaks quietly, sotto voce lean in to catch
every word pronounced lisp at once

child-like and sexy sudden laugh loud as a
stack of plates breaking

She is no classic
beauty, yet haunting in
her every imperfection.
The world drab without her,
this unbeautiful girl.

What to Keep

by CINDY CARLSON

from *HIPPOCAMPUS MAGAZINE*

The shredder's appetite is insatiable. The more I feed it, the more it whines. Paper litters the floor—tax forms, phone bills, random pages with an address or account number. Remnants of how or where my mother existed in the world make whitecaps on a beige carpet-sea.

There is one more file box. This one a heavy-duty clear plastic with a sticker announcing its contents: 1999-2005. For years it has hunkered in my closet. I trace my fingers hesitantly over its smooth red lid. Maybe it holds some long-forgotten treasure, or a special note in her own hand, or something that when I find it and tell my sister, she'll say, "Oh, that is so Mom!"

The thing about this last box, though: once it's open, it's open. When I'm finished with it, there will be no more discoveries. Every box will have been inspected, everything accounted for—either saved or gone.

I long for one more surprise, one more glimpse of her—to catch my breath for just a moment, to peek back into her world. I close my eyes, gathering the essence of her around me.

*

The day Daddy died, after the last long look from the parking lot to the second-story hospital window where we left him, after the silent drive home through the bleak March afternoon, after she pressed her fragile hand into the crook of my arm and we shuffled down the slush-caked sidewalk and up the ramp, Mom and I stepped back into the house that Daddy built. In the two days we had been gone, the simple shingled box had grown, and now it moaned and rattled in the corners. Mom, still in her frayed brown trench coat, sank into his recliner, sighed, and said, "Well, I guess it's time to move."

Looking around the living room, the hub of their home for forty years at the stack of dog-eared sheet music on the edge of the piano bench, at the dining table with the two pop-up leaves where the indentations traced every sewing project I could remember, at the built-in bookshelves where Dag Hammarskjöld and Charles Kuralt perched next to the Holy Bible and the field guides to North American birds, trees and butterflies—I wondered how we would compress the lifetime of a family of five into a space for one.

My husband and I returned the first of April—early spring in western New York, the season that never failed to break my heart. I knew there would be one or two days of delicious thaw, the snow-melt trickling in the ditches, the heady scent of a westerly breeze and red-winged blackbirds calling from pussy-willows that pushed up through the muck; but the heavy gray skies would return as always, and we would shovel, bundled in parkas called back into duty from the depths of a closet.

We taped schedules and charts to the kitchen walls; I needed to set the universe in order for the next few months, and Mom and her three out-of-town children all needed a place to channel the languor that was creeping in. The chart paper—out of place on the faded white wallpaper with the pencil-thin pale blue and avocado stripes—rustled as we squeezed past the dinette set, reminding us of the looming tasks:

1. Measure the apartment, move some big pieces, see what fits
2. Fill the new place with favorite things, make it homey
3. Stay there a few nights, see how it goes
4. Put the things no one can part with into storage
5. Pull together sellable items for a "tag sale"
6. Tackle the stuff.

All that stuff.

Mom was the original recycler. Born in 1914, the middle child of Swedish immigrant parents in a Swedish immigrant community, she grew up in the Depression and started a family during war rationing. Years later, she planned and tastefully appointed the small house her husband built on three acres along a country road, and sent three kids to college all on his school-teacher's salary. Life taught her to be frugal, practical and grounded. There was no margin for obsolescence in her world.

But it wasn't only that Mom abhorred waste; she believed everything held the potential for another purpose. With the soul of an artist and a deep appreciation for nature, craft and beauty, she could make something out of anything. So she saved everything. We grew up in a home full of objects waiting to become something else.

By the time I was a teenager, I couldn't wait to become something else. The tiny house, the homemade clothes, the rural setting all suffocated like bubble-life. Tired of sense and sensibility, most of all I wanted to not become my mother.

Rich and I finished Task #1 on that first trip. Couch, table and chairs, bed, dresser and television all jockeyed for space, then settled into the basic, one-bedroom apartment. With great flourish we checked that step off the list.

"Should I go and stay there?" Mom asked with a worried tone.

"No," I said, by now almost used to the mother-daughter role reversal. "Let's wait to do that together. No reason you can't keep staying here."

On my next trip, two weeks later, she settled on the edge of the bed in my old room among the piles of stuff-waiting-to-become. It was time for Task #6, to wade in, tackling all that latent utility with fresh green garbage bags room by room, closet by closet, drawer by drawer. Without benefit of the modern version that asks if an object is useful or brings joy to the holder, I was hoping for a compassionate, but efficient, version of purging.

"Mom, do you want this?" I asked, holding up a miniature hand-carved gnome with green pants and pointed red hat.

"Oh, I remember him," she said, and then stared past the carving in my hand. "You know, cousin Karl made that for me."

"It's sweet. Do you want it?" I handed it to her, trying to disguise my impatience at the story I'd heard so many times. At this rate she would never even see the apartment.

"I don't know," she said, "It's a shame to throw it away." She grasped the ornament between her thumb and two gnarled, arthritic fingers and let it drop to her lap.

"What about this fabric?" I asked. With a ploy not unlike one for a three-year-old, I figured I could distract her, then grab the gnome for its new home in the trash bag.

"Oh, there's that material!" she said. "I was going to make doll clothes. I think for Tina." She paused, a bit confused as to whether it was a daughter or granddaughter who would have benefitted.

"Mom, Tina is in high school."

Her head drooped; she studied the corduroy. I stopped short, suddenly ashamed of my impatience. Life was about to change. Had already changed. These piles of fabric were never to become dresses or draperies, stacks of magazines would never be enjoyed, clipped recipes would remain forever untested. She wasn't just parting with things, she was relinquishing plans and ideas. Dreams.

During her nap I decided to tackle the sewing drawer, third

one down in the linen closet. I tugged on the handle and its contents burst into the air like a pop-up toy from its canister. A dizzying array of thread, needles, zippers and buttons lined the bottom; the rest of the space was stuffed with rickrack. Rickrack of every imaginable color and size. Regular and scalloped, narrow and wide, extra thick, lacy, plain, all in original packaging or wrapped by the yard around two-inch by four-inch scraps of cardboard—more than enough rickrack to trim a lifetime of projects, planned and not-yet-even imagined.

Tears welled up as I slumped to the floor. "I'm so sorry, Mom." I whispered, staring at the gaping drawer. "We can't keep the rickrack."

Mom managed for two years in her new apartment in the senior living complex. With each visit I watched her shrink, her dowager's hump becoming more pronounced, her gaze increasingly fixed downward. After awhile she just left everything she needed on the countertops or scattered around on the furniture so she didn't have to bend or reach. But eventually she fell. And though she worked valiantly in her rehab program, after years of osteoporosis and now a fractured pelvis, it was clear she wasn't going back to her independent life.

Once Mom was settled in the nursing home, we brought in a few precious things from the apartment—her small writing desk, a couple of her weavings, photos, a lamp to counter the fluorescent lights, a mini CD player with a little Chopin for the mornings and Beethoven for the long nights. We dragged the room's standard-issue orange vinyl chair into the hallway and replaced it with her old brocade Queen Anne. If this was to be home for the rest of her life, it ought to feel like it, if not a smaller, sparser version.

We kept the apartment and its accompanying storage for a few more months. Although my sister and I claimed we needed a place to stay when we flew into town to visit, in truth, we dreaded losing it as a touchstone. But the end of its lease loomed; it was time to fly back "home" to clear it out. With Christmas lights strung over the walls where the pictures used to hang, we faced the next level of sorting—what to let go of, what to give away, what to keep. To the accompaniment of an old Beatles CD playing on my laptop, we piled and boxed and tossed, while we sang and laughed and wept.

Seven long years Mom lived in that one small spartan room, the wails and the smells of nursing home life closing around her like fog. By the last two years—confined to her wheelchair, then to her bed—thoughts of her house, her apartment, her treasures, and gradually even her family faded away.

One afternoon we watched a fat fluffy snowfall drift from a dull gray sky and she caught a glimpse of the photo on her windowsill.

"What's that?" she asked.

"It's Daddy," I answered, not yet used to telling her things that I wished she still knew, and wondering what is left when memory is gone.

I moved into the room with Mom the last few days of her life, sleeping on a cot and watching the rise and fall of her chest as she lingered. Our world of things dwindled to a candle, a notepad, a cup of tea, a bible, and all the accoutrements of hospice. My sister arrived, then my brother and sister-in-law, all of us taking turns keeping watch, all of us in our private dance of loving and letting go.

After, in our final triage, each of us claimed what we would take—a coffee mug, a few Christmas ornaments, the writing desk, a photo of a windmill from their dream vacation. Not quite ready to relinquish the room to its institutional state, I sat on the cold linoleum floor, stroking a nightgown I had found on a hook behind the door. The pale yellow flannel was soft and worn, trimmed in thin white rickrack.

*

The last box is empty. It held no big surprises—mostly files, rations for the shredder. I save a few random pieces of paper. Her last signed check, a note to herself describing a sunset, a newspaper clipping of their fiftieth wedding anniversary, some daily detritus of a well-lived life—stuff only meaningful to her, and, now, to me. This is my inheritance, its value solely as a portal to memory.

She would have set it all aside, thinking she might create a collage someday. For me, a special box will suffice. Maybe if it's big enough, I'll toss in that funny carved gnome. He's around here somewhere.

Buffy the Vampire Slayer Goes to Confession

by LISA EVE CHEBY

from *ANGELS FLIGHT LITERARY WEST*

We are the chosen,
                    one dies, another rises
                                        to confess:
Why would we settle?
          Clark Kent had a job.

Afterall, *this is the '90s*
O Daddy, O Watcher
beneath you,
we devour
your name-
calling: it will take more
to keep us quiet,

even sticks and stones won't work,

we keep them, next to the skillets and scarves,
next to the bones you broke,
on the cave-shelf,

in the dream-cave
we listened to the Black Madonna:

Love will lead you to your gift: *Death.*

Ripped back through the bragging mouth
of heaven to this life of demons and dishes.
We begat no sons, so turned on our final option:

          The potentials:

          if our gift is death,
          is it the thought that counts?

And yet you still invade
territory that is not yours,
guns cocked against the gunless, the sanctioned and the censored,
swearing

it's not worth it if she doesn't scream.

Can you hear us coming?

Catholic Boarding School, Six Years Old, 1943

by ELLINE LIPKIN

from *CALYX*

Two braids, clumsy and askew, made in a haste silted with worry
and salt-streaked with tears as the nuns shout into the quiet
of first light: order, order, orders. Grief, before so unknown,
starts to seed inside each knob of spine, prickling upward
to the atlas that holds the base of the head, tilting the whole world.
A wide-open sky now crams into a squared frame, dredging
for warmth. The rough hem of a uniform just covers
a knee before it scrapes the underside of a scarred desk.
Enschooled means encircled—a fence walling the green,
the calendar's wide gape around the blank months ahead.
Recitation, dictation, lockstep to a bell's clang. Learning
that somewhere in the world there is the stretch of long rivers,
the cross of new borders, and one day, a way out.

Home

by TONI ANN JOHNSON

from *SERVING HOUSE JOURNAL*

Monroe, New York, 1963

Mallory sat at the red Formica table, leaned down, and dug a forefinger behind her heel into the back of one of her new shoes. She yanked at the black patent leather. The Mary Janes remained stiff; no give. She was ten and her feet were still growing. She knew the shoes would never fit.

At Kiddie Corner, the store in town, she hadn't said a word to Velma about the pain. They were the last available pair. Soon as Mallory put them on, her stepmother's gloomy face turned sunny and she said, "Oh! Don't they look sharp?" When she asked, "Are they comfortable?" Mallory lied.

She could almost hear her feet cursing as she gazed down at them wishing she'd told the truth. She sat still as long as she could. Mallory wasn't about to mess up the pink Easter dress. It was not Easter. Easter had passed, but Velma wanted her in that dress.

Velma and her daddy took so long to get ready to go anywhere. She stared at their closed bedroom door. What were they doing in there?

She didn't mind that she'd be going out with them. Mallory liked to see new things. But she did not like that they'd be looking at a new house. It'd taken months to get used to this one and how far it was from where she lived.

Her sketchpad and pencil were next to Velma's flouncy fern on top of the oak bookshelf in the living room. She rose, and with each step, the vise-like Mary Janes bit the backs of her ankles and pinched her baby toes.

She sat back down, pad in lap, to sketch the Formica table. It was her favorite piece of furniture in the place. She helped pick it out. Before Velma came along. Drawing its simple, clean lines was soothing.

Except for the kitchen table, most of the rented cottage was filled with antiques and second hand furniture Velma collected. Ugly, in Mallory's opinion. Old stuff with ornate or wavy flourishes felt disorderly to her. She favored crispness. Precision. When she drew pictures, they were never of squiggly, sloppy things like other kids at school. She doodled tidy, even-sided shapes.

Her daddy and Velma finally emerged from the bedroom along with a shroud of smoke. He was puffing a cigarette and she was putting on pearl studs. Six months swollen, Velma waddled toward Mallory, the heels of her pumps clicking across the yellow and white linoleum.

She set her Chanel bag on the table and asked, "How do I look?"

"Nice," Mallory said.

She was being polite. Her stepmother's fully made up face did look good. Velma was glamorous, more glamorous than her mother was. The way she applied eyeliner, mascara, and lipstick enthralled Mallory. She watched her do it whenever she was allowed to. But Velma was unfashionably huge in her maternity dress. She looked off balance, like she could tip over, like she'd swallowed an enormous pumpkin.

"Well, thanks, Mal. So do you." Velma winked. "We girls have to stick together. A girl needs compliments." She shot a look at Mallory's daddy.

Mallory's eyes bounced to him. He wasn't looking. Or listening. Humming Chubby Checker's "The Twist," he removed his suit jacket from a chrome chair at the table.

"Everyone ready?" he asked, swiveling his hips.

Mallory stood. "May I bring my sketchpad, Daddy?"

"Yes, you may." He slipped his jacket on as he kept dancing.

Velma eyed him, tightlipped, and blew a gust from her nose. "We're going to look at a house, Phil, not to a museum. What does she need it for?"

"Vel." He stood still now, met her frown, and the corners of his mouth curved upwards. "She's creative, honey. It's fine."

Mallory looked down at her white ankle socks in the black shoes. She turned her lips inward and pressed them together so hard they hurt. If she smiled and Velma saw her, there'd be trouble. It wasn't often Velma didn't get her way.

*

Mallory sat in the middle of the backseat, sketchpad in her lap. She could see the country road and the trees, through the haze of cigarette smoke, and through her daddy's head and Velma's. His hair was wet with Vitalis, which didn't work too well to keep his curls slicked back, because it's for white people. Her daddy didn't have the kinkiest hair, but it wasn't without any kink at all. Velma's hair was pressed and curled. She knew what she was doing.

Their car pulled up and stopped directly behind a metallic-blue Chevy Impala parked at the bottom of a steep blacktop driveway below a house that sat up above the street.

"Bet that's the agent's car," Velma said.

Mallory liked cars. Some were works of art. She recognized the Chevy as a 1961 or a '62, not the newest model, but pretty close. Her daddy's 1959 Chrysler was older, and in Mallory's estimation, a less dazzling, robin's egg blue. She knew he could've bought a recent model, too, if he really wanted one. She also knew Velma was especially good with money. She worked for a Wall Street Bank before she started growing that gourd in her gut.

"Don't buy a brand new car, Phil," Mallory had heard Velma say. "Cars depreciate. You're better off buying one that's a year or two old. A house—now *that* appreciates."

Why couldn't they be satisfied with the house they already had? Mallory had finally stopped having scary dreams when she slept there. *Anxiety dreams*, Daddy had called them. They were dreams about being left somewhere, alone, and trying to find her way home.

She sketched the Chevy's backside, carefully rendering its straight lines and elegant geometric design. She hoped her daddy would turn and notice how well she was doing it.

He climbed out of the car.

And at that moment, Mallory looked up. Through the windshield she saw the real estate agent sitting in his car. He lifted his head to peer into his rear view mirror. Their cars were parked so close she saw his eyes reflecting back at her. His head spun around. He looked over his shoulder and stared through his back window at her daddy as he walked past the front of their car toward Velma's door.

The real estate man had a widow's peak and a heart shaped face that reminded Mallory of a white Valentine she made sometime after her daddy left, and her mother wouldn't buy any red construction paper. She'd used typing paper. The man was a caricature artist's dream. Caricatures made Mallory recoil. Exaggerated details were unbecoming. Still, she watched his Valentine-face closely. He squinted at the three of them.

Her daddy was busy helping Velma out of the car. She needed a tug to stand up.

The man threw open his Chevy door and jumped out.

"Well, hello, hello," he chirped, smiling at Mallory's daddy and Velma. "Nice to see you folks." He waved, sticking an arm out in a starched white shirt. "If you'll wait right here for me just a moment, please, I'm going to pop in and be sure the seller's ready. Just one moment. Be right back."

Mallory watched him hike up the bottom part of the driveway in a few giant steps. The slope of it was practically perpendicular, like an "L" that had tipped over clockwise so the horizontal part became vertical. He stopped at the top where it leveled out, caught his breath, and then trotted down the last few yards of the driveway to the house.

Her daddy and Velma didn't say anything. Mallory watched them through the windshield. They stood at the base of the driveway looking up at the house. Mallory couldn't see it too well from inside the car.

Why did they have to live up in the boonies anyway? Before Daddy and Velma moved to this town they lived in the Bronx where Mallory lived, too, and sometimes she saw him during the week. Sometimes they went for ice cream or for a Coke, even on school nights. When he and Velma moved from their apartment and rented the small house in this small town, Mallory had her own room. She'd grown to like it, but now she only saw him on weekends twice a month. Why'd he want to live some fifty miles away? Didn't he miss her? If he bought a house, that meant he'd probably never move back to the Bronx.

She realized her heart was thump-thumping in her chest really fast. She took a deep breath, and focused back on sketching. She studied the chrome bumper and breathed. It was shiny as a mirror. So shiny you could've flossed your teeth in it. As she filled in its details—three little round lights on both sides and a keyhole—Mallory wondered how much a person would have to love a thing to keep it polished like that?

Her daddy and Velma didn't let her finish the sketch. They made her get out to look at the house. Argh! Every step in those awful shoes was torture. They squished her toes and sawed grooves into her heels. She would've worn her Keds, but, no, Velma said they had to make a good impression.

Mallory moved slowly as she climbed the steep driveway. Her daddy walked backwards and pulled on Velma's hands to help her to the top. He wore a light blue shirt without a tie under his navy suit. Velma asked him to wear a tie, but he did what he wanted. Velma sewed her maternity dress herself. It had a matching jacket that was the same baby blue as his shirt. She wanted a boy. Daddy said he didn't need another kid. He said he could do without the responsibility, but if they were going to have one, he preferred a boy, too. Mallory figured this must be the reason for all the blue. Velma made sure the color flattered her skin tone. That woman did everything she could to look good. Her hair, nails, and makeup were always done. Mallory suspected she hated being fat with that stupid pumpkin. How could she not, especially after her daddy let it slip that he missed her hourglass figure?

Velma was prettier than her mother *before* the pumpkin. *During* the pumpkin, when Daddy came to get her every other week, he'd look at her mother and tell her she looked nice. Her mother liked compliments, but not from him since he left her. She never said thank you. She rarely even bothered to say goodbye. Sometimes, she'd close the door while he was still talking. He said she was rude. Mallory didn't say a thing. He wasn't dragging her into their grown up business.

When Velma got to the top of the driveway, she looked at the house and sighed. "It's so pretty," she said.

"That's called a colonial style, Mallory," Daddy told her. "You like it?" He petted her head, like she was a puppy. Velma had washed and set her hair, so it was smooth.

Mallory nodded, but she didn't know if she liked it or not. You couldn't know if a house was good or bad just by looking at the outside. That told you nothing about how it felt to live in it. You needed to learn its details. Details mattered. They mattered in art and in real life things, too.

"See the separate entrance?" Velma pointed to a metal side door. "That's gotta be the room they said you could use as an office."

Mallory's daddy lit a cigarette. He inhaled and nodded as he exhaled. "If we were to get it, looks like there's space to add on, too."

Velma lifted her shoulders toward her cheeks and smiled at him with her whole face. She smiled at him as if Mallory wasn't even there.

Her heart was beating fast again and her feet were in agony. She took a big breath in, then blew it out. She couldn't stop them from moving. What could she ever do to make Daddy do what she wanted? Nothing.

Mallory faced the house. What would it be like to live there? She had to admit the outside was attractive. Simple. It was a clean rectangle, two-toned, white over a brick bottom. She made a rough sketch. The lines weren't as interesting as the Chevy Impala's, but she preferred its plainness to the larger, older looking homes on either side. Those had excess flourishes like over-hanging roofs, and balconies, wrap around porches and shutters. This one was smaller, simpler, but it was gigantic compared to where she lived with her mother. She sketched herself in front of the house. Then she added Daddy beside her with his arm around her.

Her mother would seethe if he and Velma bought this house. And Mallory would have to listen to it. Daddy never bought her and her mother a house. Velma got to quit her job. Her mother had to work. Her mother seemed to enjoy teaching, but she still complained to Mallory about the effort it took to support them. Velma had it easy.

Velma was the one who insisted they needed a bigger house. Her lousy pumpkin was coming and she wanted Mallory's daddy to, "*Stop talking about starting your therapy practice and go ahead and start it.*" But in the house they were renting, Mallory's room had billowy white curtains on a sunny window, and she woke to birds singing, and no sirens or honking horns. She didn't need any more changes. At first the neighbors didn't like them being in that house. But at least they stopped egging their car and yelling slurs. One man even came over and told her daddy he was sorry. Other neighbors started being nicer after that.

A high-pitched yelp and laughter turned Mallory around. She saw a couple of white girls in sweatshirts and dungarees playing hopscotch up the block. Leafy maple trees lined the sidewalk. At the other end of the block, on the corner, there was a waterfall. Mallory could faintly hear it going: Swishhhhhhhhhhhhhh.

"Beautiful. Isn't it?" Velma asked, when she saw her looking. "Like a fairytale. A dream."

It was early April and not hot outside, especially with all the shade trees, but Velma was perspiring. Before she started carrying that bump of hers, she wore Chanel No.5, and she smelled elegant. She couldn't stand perfume while she had that thing in her belly, and without it, her sweat smelled a bit like a holiday ham.

Velma plucked the cigarette from between Mallory's daddy's lips, puffed on it, and then stuck it back.

Mallory turned away, back to the house. She saw a small face appear in the middle window on the top floor. A little kid's face. She wasn't sure if it was a boy or girl. It had hair like a black poodle's, which was similar to her own when it wasn't straightened. The face saw her see it, and then ducked from the window.

The real estate man came back through the front door wearing a grim look on his heart-shaped face. "Bad news," he said. He made clicking sounds as he shook his head right, left, right. "Now, we can take a look, you did come all the way here, but it turns out this house is in escrow. I'm sorry."

"What?" Velma said. She sucked her teeth and crossed her arms above her pumpkin.

"But not to worry," he said. "There's another house available across town."

"I researched *this* house," Velma said. "And this is the one I wanna see. We just spoke this morning." Her voice got louder. "It went into escrow since *then*?"

The man tugged his ear. "Apparently," he said. "Sorry about that."

Velma lowered her chin and stared him in the eye. "This house better really be in escrow, because we will check."

"And we do have a lawyer," Mallory's daddy said. He put a hand on Velma's lower back.

"Uh, you folks—." The man's face went pink. He smiled and winced at the same time. "Now, I think you've got the wrong idea, here. I'm told the house is in escrow. But, uh, as I said, we can take a look. There's always a chance it could fall out of escrow."

Velma rolled her eyes and exhaled.

The man pulled at his collar and cleared his throat.

Mallory watched her daddy. He was silent. He stared at the man, and smoked.

"Mr. Arrington, you'll have to put your cigarette out before we go in."

"It's Doctor Arrington," he said. He eyed the man and did not look away.

"That's great. Would you please put your cigarette out?"

"Did you call me over here to look at a house that's apparently in escrow?"

The man didn't answer.

"You can wait until I'm finished."

Mallory saw the man blink a whole bunch of times and then blow air through his lips. He must have blown through his nose, too, because a booger peeked out and dangled there. Disgusting. No one told him. Velma looked at Mallory and squinched up her face. They both smiled. Mallory could have sketched that booger face perfectly, but she didn't draw gross things.

When her daddy finally crushed his cigarette on the driveway, he stuck the butt into his box of Benson & Hedges. The three of them followed the man inside.

Velma wanted to see the room with the separate entrance. It had a checkered floor. Black and white. Shadow and light. Chiaroscuro. Mallory learned that in an art book. The room also had built-in bookshelves, and a bathroom with a toilet and a sink. A "half bathroom," Velma called it.

She said, "Oh, this is perfect, Phil. Don't you think? For your office?"

"Would be if it were available."

The booger-man stood in the doorway, and Mallory's daddy eyed him like he wanted to mush him flat with the bottom of his shoe.

The man looked down at his black loafers.

The kitchen, dining room, and living room were up a short staircase; the bedrooms, on the top floor, up a longer staircase. The dining room and living room were grand T-shaped space with an extra high ceiling. Mallory could see the upstairs hallway from there because the hallway was also a balcony that overlooked the dining area.

Velma looked up at the balcony, put a hand on her pumpkin, and said, "Oh. That's lovely."

Two white men in plaid shirts were sitting at a mahogany dining table that faced a large window with a view of a forsythia bush in the backyard that looked like cloud of bright-buttered-popcorn. The men turned and nodded a greeting. They didn't speak. Velma and Mallory's daddy waved, as they followed the booger-man through a swinging door into the kitchen. Mallory lagged behind.

One man was old and round, with short white hair on his head and a little poking out of his ears. The other was much younger and skinny, with long dark curls. He had a beard, too. There were crumbs in it. They were drinking coffee and munching on matzo.

The older man turned to look at her. He smiled. "Well aren't you a little beauty?" he said. "And don't you look nice today in your pretty pink dress?" His voice was kind. "Would you like a cracker, darling?" The way he said crackah and dahlink reminded Mallory of her mother's butcher in the Bronx.

She nodded. "Yes, thank you."

He handed her a big square of matzo. Matzo was like a giant Saltine without the salt. She figured he thought she wouldn't know what it was called, but they had matzo in the Bronx.

Velma and Mallory's daddy came back through the swinging door. Velma said to be careful not to get any crumbs on the floor.

The older man glanced down at the Oriental rug, shrugged, and said, "Don't worry about it, dahlink." He raised an arm behind him, toward the balcony. "Please. Go up. Have a good look."

The younger man said his niece was in the middle bedroom, but to tap on the door.

When booger-man started up the stairs, the older man turned and said, "Why don't you wait here?"

The booger-man looked back at him.

"Why work so hard? If they have questions," the old man's hand rose toward the balcony. "We can see them from here."

They locked eyes for a moment. Booger-man raised his eyebrows and smiled at the man. He nodded. "Okay, sure," he said, and he thumped back down the steps.

The old man picked up a paper napkin and held it out. "For your nose," he said. "Blow it. Please. My appetite begs you."

The bathroom was at the top of the stairs. The medicine cabinet was long and mirrored, and it had sliding doors. The wall tiles, tub, and toilet were shiny pink. They matched Mallory's dress perfectly. It was a sign that she belonged there!

Velma said, "It's great. Isn't it, Phil?"

He nodded and turned to Mallory. "Plenty of room for your hair products, huh, Mal?" He chuckled and rubbed her back.

"Plenty of room for *baby* things," Velma said, as if she were correcting him. "That counter has room to change a diaper."

"Velma, that counter has room to change a grown man's underwear. There's space for Mallory's things, too."

"I guess," she said. "Sure is a lot of space."

Mallory wanted to pull those horrible shoes off and hurl one at her stepmother. The backs of her ankles felt raw. And she was sure her baby toes had blisters.

The smallest bedroom was closest to the bathroom. All that fit in there was a single bed, a nightstand, and a dresser. Her daddy and Velma didn't say anything when they looked inside.

The middle room's door was closed. Velma knocked and the curly haired girl opened it. She had a Barbie in her hand. Mallory could tell by the smell that it was new. She loved the powdery, plastic smell of a brand new Barbie. The little girl smiled and wiggled a loose front tooth with her tongue. Then she sat down with the rest of her dolls on the floor. The room had a bed, a desk, a bookcase, dresser, and a play table with a tea set on it.

"This would be perfect for the baby, Phil," Velma said.

"Yeah. *If* the house were to fall out of escrow," he whispered.

"We'll see about that," Velma said.

"So, that first room would be mine, right?" Mallory asked.

"Yes, when you're here, Mallory," Velma said. "It would be

yours and the guest room. And it'll have the prettiest curtains in the whole house, and the nicest bed linens. Just like you have now."

What? Her room was really the guest room? She wanted to look at her daddy to see if this was true. But she couldn't, because her eyes welled up and she didn't want him to see.

Would the pumpkin have to share its room with guests, too? Probably not.

This was a detail that made a difference.

So, she'd have to share her daddy *and* her room? And the pumpkin would get to have Daddy all week, every week, and a bigger room of its own?

Apparently.

She followed them down the hall to the last door. The master bedroom was the largest, but not that great. She barely bothered to look.

When they went outside and made it down to the bottom of the driveway and their cars, the real estate agent said, "So, shall we take a look at the other house?"

Mallory's daddy turned to Velma.

She looked at the agent. "We like *this* one."

The man exhaled. "Right. And if it comes back on the market, you'll be first to know. In the meantime there's a place for sale across town. Here's the address." He handed her daddy a slip of paper. "You know how to get across the Erie Line to Spring Street?"

"Across the tracks?" he asked, like *are you kidding me?*

The man crossed his arms. "Look, it's up to you. It's a nice house. You want to see it, make the right on Spring, and keep going about a quarter of a mile," he said. He slipped into his shiny Chevy and drove off.

Her daddy opened the car door for Velma. She didn't get in. She looked all around, and then finally she stared at the waterfall down the street. The water poured from a large pond, angled over a straight ledge of rocks, and plunged into a flowing stream.

"Velma, what are you doing?" he asked.

"I'm thinking," she said.

She was listening, too. Her eyes were closed and her head was tilted back a little. Mallory had seen that exact look on her face once when she listened to one of her daddy's opera records.

Mallory climbed into the car. She didn't feel like sketching anymore. She didn't feel like doing anything but taking those damned shoes off. Why should she care about any new house?

All she was going to get was a guest room. She was the weekend kid. Velma's pumpkin could rot. What did it do to deserve its own room and to live with her daddy in a big house?

Velma fell into her seat with a thud. Mallory's daddy got in and started the car.

Then the young, bearded, skinny man from the dining room came sprinting out of the house, waving his arms. "Wait!" he yelled. "Please, wait!"

Her daddy turned the engine off and rolled down the window.

The man ran to the bottom of the driveway, sliding a bit in his sneakers. "Listen," he said, short of breath as he approached the car window. "We didn't want to tell you in front of the agent, but you should know that he came in before you and said, 'These colored people wanna see your house. Legally, I have to show it to them, but I'll tell 'em it's in escrow.' My father wants you to know he's not like that. He says if you wanna buy this house, he'll be happy to sell it to you."

Velma covered her face with her hands.

"Thank you," Mallory's daddy said. He looked at Velma and put a hand on her thigh. "Well?"

She plucked a Kleenex from her Chanel bag and dabbed her eyes. "Tell your father, we'll take it," she said.

The man nodded. "Would you like to come back in and look around some more?"

"Yes," Velma said, sniffling.

"But the real estate man thinks you'll meet him at the other house," Mallory said. She pictured him and his Valentine face standing there, waiting.

Velma turned and looked at her. She laughed, even as she was crying.

Her daddy smiled. "Don't worry about him, Mallory."

Velma blew her nose. She kept crying and laughing as she lifted her swollen self out of the car.

The skinny man began to help Mallory's daddy haul her up the driveway.

"I'll wait in the car," Mallory muttered. She was already unbuckling the straps on her shoes.

"No, baby. You come with us," he said, looking back at her. "Come on, now."

They reached the top of the driveway and she watched him hold Velma's hand. They were waiting for her.

She didn't want to go. Her feet hurt so much and it wouldn't be any fun. But they'd keep waiting and if she didn't do as she was told they'd yell or come get her or maybe even punish her. There was no choice. So she would go. She'd go in and she'd sketch her new room the way *she* wanted it to be. She'd put herself, and all her things inside it. They'd fit perfectly. And it wouldn't be a guest room, ever, even when she wasn't there. Because she wasn't a guest! She'd draw everything she could think of. Daddy would be there, tucking her into her own bed, with her own linens. There'd be no pumpkin. Just her. She'd draw every detail, exactly the way she wanted it. And she'd keep drawing and drawing and drawing until it finally felt like home.

The Women Who Love Me

by LACOYA KATOE GESSESSE

from *TIFERET*

The women who love me speak of their lives in past tense. They show me unfulfilled dreams balled between fingers they refuse to unfurl. What glimpses I get of them ooze out between their knuckles, snippets of who they might have been had they broken free. Before I put the pieces of their lives together, they snatch back these possibilities and hold them against their chests. "Too late for me," they say, "but you still have time." They lay pressure upon my heart like boulders; I must carry their burdens and my own. But the work of transformation is mine alone to do. They don't tell me that in order to transform, I'll nudge our boulders a centimeter at first, then an inch, and every time I think I've done work enough to slip from under them, they fall on me again. But I do my work—repetitively—in different cities, on different jobs, in the arms of different lovers. I celebrate the smallest victories and try not to tally my losses. When the boulders grow heavy again, I make new attempts at freedom, always praying palms up, fighting the urge to clasp my fingers around anyone I might become.

Dear Intimacy of [Theory]

by MURIEL LEUNG

from *WILDNESS*

Dear ____________________________ intimacy of [theory]____,

Of which I make grooves in my skirt imagining all possibilities for wandering. These are the most precious parts of my days. When the forest can decamp without me, the place fleeing the person. I want to write these possibilities the way trees can rush forth into its most unknowable entanglements. Root defying root in its bind. In a sense, this is a love letter in which I, now forestless, am seeking you in the swarm. When I say [intimacy] I do not mean that every experience within me is forageable. I mean that a certain care can hold the water still enough and it is teeming with life. In bell hooks' terms, [theory] as "location for healing" / "theory as intervention" makes the living something worthy of amassing. That is all I want. Your gratuitous sorrows falling out a bell sleeve, asking, *How do I repair?* Even as your sorrows parrot other sorrows.

Together and Far, Far Apart

by MURIEL LEUNG

from *GULF COAST*

You in your resplendent prose
Me in my wilding and tumbleweed syntax
You and the spackled floors of a harbinger house
Me and my trinity of holes
You in the tiger cage
Me in my pile of keyholes set on fire
How you say the world is a hopeless box of maggot-meat and
  hungry men go to war
How I am poor and thread a colossus through a needle eye
How you splendor and eat to your heart's content
How I wreck myself with very little
When you tell me *Jump!* I say, *Achoo!* and turn to defiant dust
When I ask you kindly, *Please undress me* you are touching a white
  wall with pornographer hands
When you ask me if I will marry, I pluck the toenails from your toes
There is so much laughter I do not realize I am bending towards
  the sun
When I fall in love, you turn into a ladder I am not allowed to
  climb
I climb the ladder anyway and it takes me into a land of
  whalebones
You say, *Have you learned your lesson now?*
I bite my lip and harden myself to coal
These are the ways you stop a blood sack from leaking
These are the terms by which I move and you move quicker

The Upholsterer

by DÉSIRÉE ZAMORANO

from *KENYON REVIEW*

Enrique looked at his cousin and at the sofa that had just landed in his workshop.

The couch was a sodden mess covered in food stuffs, and Enrique really didn't want to know about it, nor did he have any expectations of what he would find underneath the fabric. Probably a factory assembled pieces of cheap teak wood with low grade stuffing and springs.

His cousin had set it down in Enrique's work space with a flourish, like he had just delivered some kind of previous cargo or gift, and then started talking some crazy shit about the San Gabriel Valley. Enrique shook his head, ignored Gilbert, and evaluated the piece of crap in front of him. He expected the cushion seat to be land fill when he ripped it; but he liked the lines of the sofa. He'd make his decision when he opened it up, examined its springs and its bones.

"I don't know," Gil insisted. "Thought you could make some money on it, you know? This girl I know was just gonna throw it out."

Enrique nodded his head, then glanced at Gilbert, whose insistent presence was making him edgy. Enrique's eyes narrowed, why was he still here?

"You want a coffee? A beer?"

"Nah, cousin, I just wanted to give this to a good home. Maybe you can get a good price for it."

Enrique, doubting it profoundly, made a sour face, then realized why this young man hovered. "Thank you, Gil," Enrique said.

Gilbert dipped his head, clambered back into his tow truck, and drove off.

The sofa sat there in a provocative silence.

If he left the wet fabric covering it, even if it had beautiful wood it could warp. Enrique ran his hands through his hair, he needed to get it trimmed, the gray was overtaking the black, and a sharp razor cut would help convince Javier that he was still a youngish man, not young like Gil, but not an old man, yet.

He reached for his staple remover, started feeling around at the webbing of the base, then the platform and was pleasantly surprised to find there were no staples. He nodded to himself. Now the odds of finding kiln fired wood were not certain but better.

Now he reached for his ripping chisel with the shouldered tang and his wooden mallet. The gentle approach would take much longer, but he had a sense it would be worth it.

He had wanted to simply strip the fabric, any lining, to ensure that the wood underneath wouldn't become damaged by the moisture. Instead he found himself pulling of the fabric and removing the stuffing. The springs had been hand tied, eight times. There was no trace of glue, the wood interlocked beautifully. And the wood was kiln fired. Enrique was impressed with his cousin's find. This piece was all show wood and had beautiful bones.

It reminded him of Javier.

The stuffing thoroughly removed, the springs inspected, the wood admired, Enrique returned his tools to where they belongs, carried the destroyed fabric to the side of his workshop and threw it all into the dumpster.

Inside his home he showered off the sweat of exertion and avoided thinking about Javier in Vancouver. Drying himself off with a worn gray towel he inspected himself in the mirror. He knew what he saw in Javier, the fine bones, the dark laughing eyes, that sweet scent of his; and what did he have? Gray hair sprouting in alarming places, a face of pouches, eyes that glared red.

He'd have gone to Vancouver if he could.

That evening Enrique lay in his bed and listened to the sounds of the freeway rushing by. He listened until it slowed, faded, and he heard no more.

Enrique's shop was the garage of his home. The sofa arrived between jobs; Enrique had just finished up the enormous task of recovering an elaborate dining set that would ultimately find its home in a palatial dining room inside a Chatsworth gated community.

He worked only by word of mouth and was never without work for long. Many of his finely wrought pieces could be found throughout Southern California, from Brentwood to Corona Del Mar. His clients had paid his home here, and a home for his mother in another world, for him another planet, Teotitlan de Valle.

Best not to think on that.

He crossed when he was 15.

Would he have stayed if he knew he wouldn't be able to return?

Would he have?

Now he spoke more English than Zapotec, and less Zapotec than Spanish. Not enough room in his head for everything, and while learning this trade from a Russian born in Minsk he learned English and Yiddish.

He texted his mother every few days, and sent her money every week, spoke to her on Sunday mornings.

Sending the money was his ritual, his belief that she would live forever.

He hated to think of that, she would not live forever, so when would he see her again?

The first time Javier showed him how to Skype with her, was a disaster. Something was wrong on her end and they didn't have anyone there would could help. Then one of Enrique's many nieces, Demetria, made it work and there they were, all of them, in the concrete home Enrique's money had built. There was his mother smiling down into the screen, laughing at it all and Enrique got so choked up he couldn't speak.

Did the camera distort her face? Or had it sagged and flattened and spread in the time he had last seen her. He could only watch her, he couldn't touch her or feel her and for days afterwards there was and ache in his chest as if his ribs were broken. As if he were broken.

"So go visit," Javier said, with a young man's ease and the entitlement of a US passport.

He was too old to make that trip north a second time. The first time, nearly forty years ago, at 15, had almost killed him.

No, he would not do that again.

"Why don't you get legal?" Javier had asked him. The depth of ignorance that question betrayed threatened to uncouple his emotions for him.

"How?" he has asked, icily.

"Talk to an attorney."

At which point Enrique coldly lay out the various legal routes for immigration, none of which applied to him, a single man, who owned his own business.

Javier frowned in a way that destroyed Enrique's anger and said, "I always thought there was a way, dude."

Too beautiful, too young to realize that not every dream is possible.

The bones of the abandoned sofa tugged at him, like Javier, he thought. Did Javier need furniture? Did his own living room need a piece of folly—to displace the winged arm chairs he had so tenderly revived? To guard his meager coffee table and gaze at a blank wall?

The empty days stretched into an empty week and Enrique filled it with the project of this couch. If he couldn't find the right home for it, he'd put it in his living room. He felt the itch of this wood beckon him, and without a client to please or to accommodate, he had a design in mind.

(Had it been 30 years since he felt her touch, her breath on his face, her eyes on his face, her light touch on his arm, her love on his skin? Had it been forty years, and why could he not stop thinking about it? Was this is an omen, a foreshadowing, was she leaving this world? Was she calling him back?)

He would call her in the morning. He would talk to her. He would remember that he had been hearing her voice each week, and its gradual descent into the voice of an older woman he had never met. He loved her, it was all right, she knew he loved her. The checks proved that, her home proved that, his work proved that.

A raw ache continued to spread inside him, as if his ribs were shards of glass.

He was getting old. He was getting sentimental. This was stupid.

The price of his home on a rough lot in El Monte would have shocked his family in el Valle. They celebrated his success, however, with packages from home filled with food stuffs that made it through, small gifts, carved, woven, painted. But what touched him the most was the tapestry his mother and her sisters had woven, the colors of his childhood, the colors of his home town, the colors of the skirt and the embroidery on the blouses the women wore.

He rubbed his hand across the fabric. He felt the texture of the weave, the compact threading. He examined the stitching of the embroidery. He examined the structure of the furniture again.

At least this dream was achievable.

A designer texted him and he ignored it. An upholstered head board, a dining set, a quien sabe que—he ignored it.

Javier called, and they spoke, Javier had quite a bit of work in Vancouver, he wouldn't be back as soon as he thought.

Enrique closed his eyes against this. Was it a lie? Was it a gentle dismissal?

He had never been a jealous man, he had navigated his passions with a stoic equanimity, a sense that people arrived and people disappeared, just as he had, and inevitably so would they. But now that he was in his fifties, he felt himself grasping for Javier, hoping to hold him close, fast, and for good.

Enrique knew Javier was a young man. How much longer could this last?

The fabric from his home town would not of course be enough for an entire cushion, much less the piece. But he knew what he wanted.

He measured, he ordered online. He adjusted the springs. When the distressed leather arrived he measured, sewed then stitched. He double checked the linings for the distressed leather. He measured, cut, stitched. He spent an entire afternoon regulating the stuffing, ensuring its firmness to what he had in mind.

He embedded the talisman of his home town in the center of the sofa back, a vibrant contrast with the tanned leather.

When he was done he paced around it, examining the base, to verify that his handiwork was invisible, admiring the stitching on the leather seams he had added as a decorative element; he sat down and found himself pleased with the firmness; he leaned back and felt the gentle brush of fabric behind his head.

He stood and examined it with his skeptical professional eye, and decided he had done well. With the help of a dolly and drop cloths he wheeled it into his living area, pushing aside the arm chairs, moving the stacks of circulars and junks mail into the trash, and gently lowering the new couch to the floor, maneuvering it until Enrique felt it was in its rightful place.

He stood across from it, and nodded at the shape, at the vibrancy of the fabric, at the completion of his work. "Good," he said.

After he showered he drove a few blocks and picked up a torta and some fries and brought them home. He ate in silence at his dining table and admired the back of his new sofa. He texted with his mother; they would talk tomorrow, Sunday morning at 9 a.m., as usual.

He cleaned up after himself, throwing out the leftover scraps of food, the packaging, wiping down his simple tables. He washed and dried his hands, he didn't want greasy finger prints on his new piece of furniture.

He sat down on it, and approved. He stretched across it, grabbing a cushion he had made, also from his home town fabric, propped it under his head, and closed his eyes.

He listened to the traffic noise of the highway; to the distant barking of a lonely dog, and its loneliness made him think of Javier, and how they had not spoken in a week. He had done this work for him, Enrique realized. He had hoped this would be a gift, like a grand gesture. He was certain that, instead, it would stay in his living room.

He thought of his brother and sisters with their families in el Valle. He had not wanted their lives. Did he want this one?

You make yourself crazy. In the States, everyone made themselves crazy, he had noticed. They don't even know they're doing it—and now he was turning into one of them, fully American.

The pain in his chest increased. This was his life. This was who he was. This was who he would remain.

That was the refrain the circled in his head, and at the same time he swore he could catch the scent of his mother, the scent of wool across a loom. He closed his eyes.

When he awoke he lay a moment on the sofa before opening his eyes. He felt an unusual warmth across his body and thought it might be sun streaming in—he heard the familiar squawking of a distant rooster, but the highway was silent. Was it Sunday already? He had to get ready for his call.

He opened his eyes and became immediately disoriented. He was laying on his sofa, but no longer in his living room, he was in the bright outdoor sunshine.

What kind of prank was this? Had someone moved him in his sleep? Was he drunk? Medicated? Having an attack of the nerves?

He blinked against the light up into an unfamiliar shade of blue sky; glancing around he saw that they were against a building.

He inhaled—there was no longer a trace of diesel, a whisper of salt. He inhaled the scent of the earth.

He stood, a little unevenly and the view of the valley was like a blow to his sternum: he knew that valley from childhood—although the buildings and acres of fields must have exploded four times at least. He looked around wildly. He knew where he was, and he didn't care how he had gotten there.

He moved around the building, and saw the concrete structure that now replaced the walls of wood he had grown up in.

"Amá, Amá" he said, and strode off in search of her.

From inside the building he heard her welcoming response, "Shiñé, Shiñé"

*

Javier parked in Enrique's drive. He was tired from the flight, and a bit irritated that Enrique hadn't returned his calls. So moody! So emo! Javier had once thought natives were stoic, silent, people who never betrayed their emotions. Kiki did, with a tiny movement on his mouth Javier could read the multifaceted range of his emotions:

disapproval, need, tenderness, relief.

Enrique adored him, and, in return, Javier found himself, despite the age difference, loving him. With Enrique, Javier at last felt calm, soothed, desired and loved.

You could love someone and still be annoyed by their moodiness, thought Javier and he tramped up the steps, and rapped sternly on the front door.

Silence.

Javier unhitched his messenger bag from his shoulder, dug around into it and pulled out his set of keys. Kiki was such a funny old man, the way he had given him a set of keys, as if he had presumed too much.

Javier unlocked the dead bolt, retrieved his bag and stepped in.

"Kiki?"

Javier spotted him, asleep on a new couch. For a moment Javier admired the furniture, it would have to have been his work to have been elevated into this prominent place in the home. He crept up to it, silently. The leather was a weathered deep tan, as dark as Enrique, with a spectacularly colored swatch of fabric working into it. Javier noticed that Enrique hugged a pillow made out of the same fabric, as if in an embrace.

"Hey, hey, Kiki," Javier said gently. It was, after all, the afternoon. "Wake up, viejito."

Javier stood over him, waiting. On Kiki's face was a smile of peace and contentment. "Sweet dreams, old man, I can't wake you while you're so happy," Javier tousled his hair, then stood abruptly.

Enrique would not awake again.

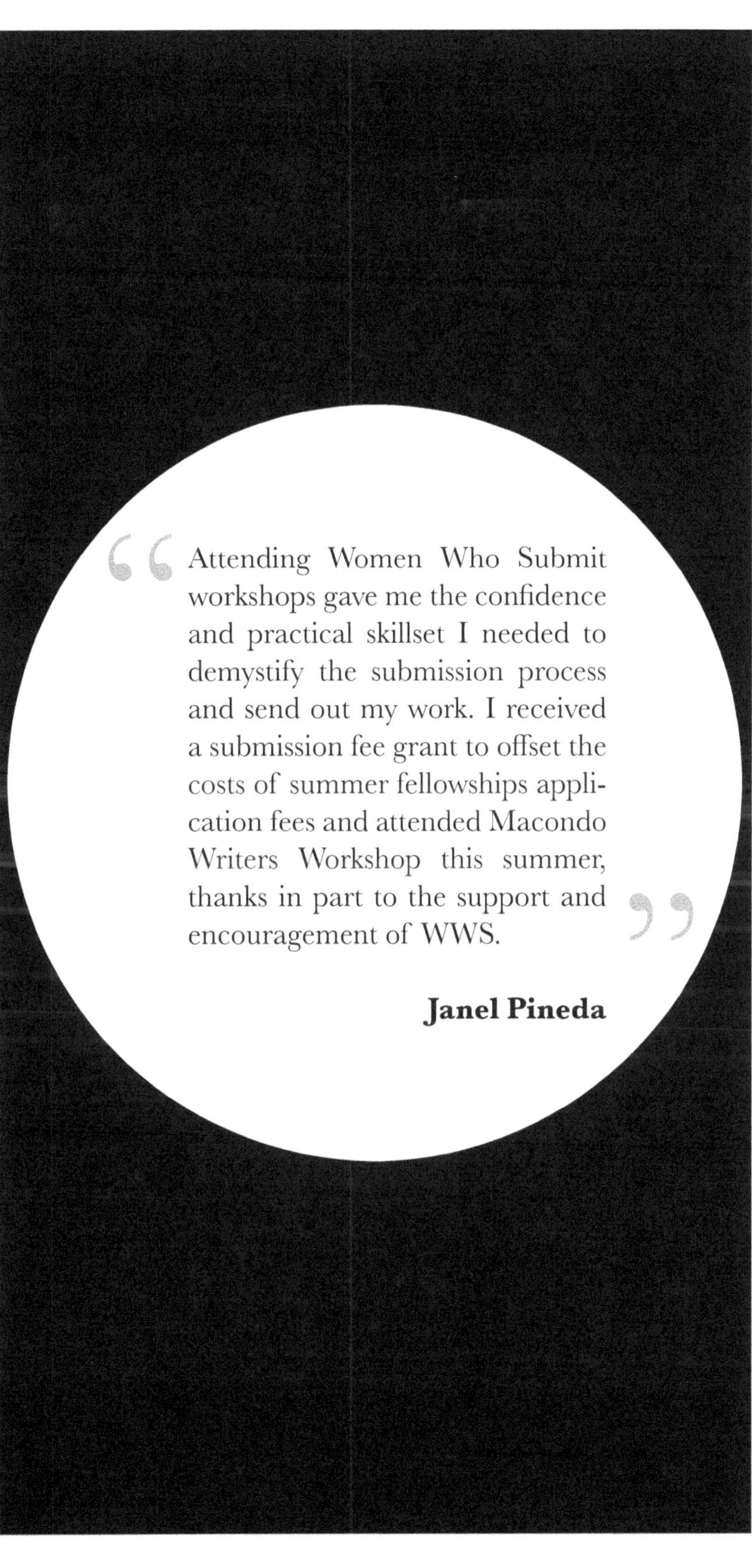
"Attending Women Who Submit workshops gave me the confidence and practical skillset I needed to demystify the submission process and send out my work. I received a submission fee grant to offset the costs of summer fellowships application fees and attended Macondo Writers Workshop this summer, thanks in part to the support and encouragement of WWS."
Janel Pineda

When You're Poor

by HEATHER ROMERO-KORNBLUM

from *SPARKLE & BLINK*

When you're poor and you drop the $4 salsa container
you stare at the splatter pattern on the floor
and count the losses in dollars and cents

You buy your son a fancy Larabar, and when he doesn't finish it
you eat it and hope you don't catch his cold

You pour the liquid from the squash you roasted into the soup
and pour the excess soup broth into the rice you cook

You keep your head down and don't talk to people
You don't react to the Facebook status of an acquaintance, who shares
that she needs extra frequent flier miles to get back early from her $2,000 vacation
because her dad is dying
Maybe you become a shitty friend

You don't ask your landlord to fix things
You don't fix your car
You don't get the bump you have under your eyelid checked out,
even though you have health insurance

You keep stocking your pantry with cans

You don't buy your son an animal balloon at the farmers market

You don't want to listen to your middle class-ish white friends
talk about why they voted third party

You cash your WIC checks at the supermarket and apologize to everyone around you
for the cashier's difficulty in understanding how to process a WIC check

You apologize again to the cashier when they yell at you
because they don't know how to process a WIC check

You simultaneously thank and apologize again to the cashier on the
    way out
and wonder why they're so angry at you
You assume the cashier is poor, too

You apologize to your son, sitting in the shopping cart, who says
"Mama, why is it taking so long?"

Your birth control fails and you get an abortion over winter break
because Obama is still President, and you still can, and your
    partner's immigration status
is precarious under the incoming regime
and you don't know what you would do if your partner were deported
and you were left with two children by yourself
You don't tell anyone

You keep your 4.0 at school
(mothers, if they do anything, have to be doing it perfectly, and never
    for the sake of success, itself)

You eat your whole lunch and your son's leftover breakfast in your
    car, at 10am,
after you drop him off at preschool

Your father thinks that your poverty is proof of your ineptitude in a
    man's world,
and you stop talking to him
(You remind yourself that he beat you when you were little.
You remind yourself that for the past 25/35 years of your life, he
    told you that
you were emasculating men by being competitive –
that you needed to watch it, or you would get fat.
He said this to you even when you were a size 0 and abusing laxatives.)

You think that you are broken and that people will always know you
    were once poor
A mark of shame written into the way you save coupons or eat food
    past the expiration date

You will always pour the liquid from the roasted squash into the soup

Comfort Food

by MIA NAKAJI MONNIER

from *SHONDALAND*

I've been chasing Japanese flavors lately: the sweetness of a matcha parfait shared with my mom, the mustard heat of hiyashi chuka, the clean nuttiness of mugicha, as Japanese as cypress wood. On days when I need comfort, nothing delivers it like this food, the food of my culture—the infinite combinations of soy and seaweed and rice.

I've been needing this kind of comfort more often lately—though I'm embarrassed to admit it. My life is easy. I have a good job, doing what I dreamed of doing as a kid. My parents are healthy. I'm healthy. Yet I can't shake the nagging feeling, embedded under my skin, that something is wrong. Often I wake to find it there, this sense that I'm falling short in ways both concrete and not: I've failed to write the story I imagined, I've failed to clean my apartment, I've failed to feel good, despite my good life. At the new ice cream shop in my neighborhood, I order the Japanese neapolitan (stripes of matcha, goma, sakura) and eat it slowly, knowing that too soon it will be gone and I will be left with the same hunger.

When I try to explain this anxiety to others, it often feels indulgent and unfriendly. Its urgency belies a dull predictability, leading to the same revelations that somehow escape me again and again. It's maddeningly nebulous, a mess of feelings and resolutions floating everywhere—and sometimes, a change of location or the taste of a certain flavor is the only way I know how to anchor myself. As a mixed-race woman, I'm particularly desperate for this anchor, for a moment to be still and whole and free from explaining myself to anyone.

I eat my feelings in the typical way, for that bloom of pleasure that briefly drowns the other noises in my brain. But with Japanese food, I'm also aware of rebuilding myself, nourishing something necessary and vulnerable that, increasingly, I have to sustain alone. I try the poke place down the street, where the Japanese owner, hearing that my mom is from Osaka, gives me a can of green tea and a scoop of fried onions. "I have to honor our blood," he says. In the restaurant's courtyard, I scribble notes I hope I can hold long enough to turn into something more.

A year ago, while I visited her in another state, a close white friend of 10 years looked me in the eyes and called me a "dirty half-breed." It was a joke, maybe. Neither of us laughed. We'd been talking about a hybrid animal, a beefalo. Which one of my parents was supposed to be the cow in this scenario, I wondered, and which one the buffalo? Later, I Googled their images, looked into their brown eyes, and considered the possible permutations, as if my friend had left a meaningful clue in the metaphor.

The moment passed as soon as it came. I stayed at my friend's house for the rest of the week as I'd planned, all but forgetting her words. And then, when she dropped me off at the Airbnb I'd booked myself for the next two nights, it all came rushing back at once. I remembered how, in college, when we'd just met, my friend had insulted my Japanese food until I'd stopped eating it around her, switching to cheese and crackers and bread with butter. Who can say no to carbs and dairy, anyway? I saved my Japanese food cravings for parties with my Asian friends. From places as far-flung as Singapore and Alaska and Hong Kong and New Hampshire, we improvised meals together with limited ingredients, my mini rice cooker the life of the party. Soon, this divided diet felt perfectly natural, my Japanese self reserved for places where it felt embraced, where it felt safe.

As I remembered this, I'd been wandering Whole Foods looking for snacks. Alone for the first time in a week, I chose the trail mix with sesame sticks, and when the South Asian cashier let me have them for free because the bar code was scratched, I wanted to hug him. That night, my Airbnb host, a Chinese-American guy named Peter, told me where to go for the best shrimp chips he'd ever had. They came free and refillable at the bar; crisp, oily, and quick to dissolve. They tasted like my childhood. I thought of the processed kind my relatives used to send from Los Angeles when we still lived in the Midwest. My brothers and I fought over them, eating as quickly as we could, our mouths and fingers smelling of shrimp essence and salt.

In those two days before returning home, I let myself chase comfort even when it felt corny, buying stationery at my favorite Japanese American-owned boutique, eating Japanese-French pastries, drinking a houjicha latte, having my nails painted a shade of raw tuna-red called Maki Me Happy. Meanwhile, I reached out to close friends and gratefully took their support. One told me about his favorite nearby sushi place, and I went there for dinner and ordered chirashi zushi. For the first time, I sat alone at the bar and chatted with the other people beside me. We talked about food and gentrification, and I spoke Japanese with the waiter, who was surprised but not too much to reply rapidfire with a smile. Every bite of the fresh local fish felt like a defiant triumph—a reclamation, a middle finger, a relief.

The high of newfound strength and community and identity lasted for a couple of months before those words—"dirty half-breed"—began coming back to me. I hear them now when I see cute mixed kids, when I edit essays about race, when I try to write an essay of my own. I think about my in-between identity—how I'm other enough to be called a "half-breed," and white enough for my offense to come as a surprise. At a lunch meeting, I order tekka maki, but it's a pale imitation.

In therapy, I talk about these things: my anxiety, the beefalo incident, my writer's block, eating. We talk about how to channel my nervous energy into constructive action. I can do it in bursts, write with abandon, eat in moderation. Then I slip again. I remember the soft Japanese cream puffs my mom eats in one bite, her smile guilty and bright with joy. My younger brothers have moved to another state and send us photos of their homemade curry in a group text. "Jozu," my mom replies, "Good job." No matter how many times my mom brings him a bento for dinner, my dad always says, "Is this for me? Thank you." I pour hot water onto rice and shiso, and watch the steam rise up. I take a bite. As long as the flavor lasts on my tongue, I have history, I have context. As long as the flavor lasts, I am not half—I am whole.

Camp Stories

by NORIKO NAKADA

from *KARTIKA*

Glass marbles in
pants pockets and
a forever
train ride rumbling
toward a mountain

shaped like a heart
keeping close watch
over barracks
coated in grit,
dust, desert sky

friends spin glass in
powdery dirt
beneath towers
beside gardens,
blocks, and school yards

where brown boys crawl
beneath barbed wire
and crack cold, dark
watermelons
across their knees

and the hearts seem
even sweeter
because for a
few moments they
are free.

Invisible Lines

by SEHBA SARWAR

from *BORDERLINES*

For the women in my lineage, who have made our homes in spaces in-between, in places we found because we had to leave or chose to shift from one city or country to another, and lived portions of our lives somewhere between those two places—the only way to feel at home is to let go while remaining connected.

*

My first flight to the US is in 1983 on a Lufthansa flight from Karachi, Pakistan to Boston via Frankfurt. Once I land, I spend a few days with my aunt, my mother's cousin in Cambridge, Massachusetts after which I clamber onto Greyhound and Peter Pan buses that transport me to South Hadley, where I attend Mount Holyoke College. After graduation, while preparing to return to Karachi, I cram my down jacket, duck boots, pillows, and comforter into boxes that I leave (and never see again) at my aunt's Cambridge house, and return to Karachi with even less than I brought to college. But before packing, I ship my books—by Chinua Achebe, Nadine Gordimer, Bapsi Sidhwa and more—to Karachi. After all, college is where I discover that a writer can be brown or black and produce work in English; in my Karachi English-medium school where I take Cambridge exams, only read works by Shakespeare and nineteenth-century British writers.

But a few years later, while enrolled in graduate school in Austin, Texas, I meet and fall in love with a Chicano educator René, who was born in Brownsville, Texas on the US-Mexico border and is also connected to two sides of a forced line. When René is offered a position in Houston's public education system, I follow, stashing my cat, books, bedcovers, and clothes in my Honda hatchback. And I, like my parents' families, who in the 1950s moved from India to Pakistan with no long-term plans, remain in Texas for more than 20 years, during which time I give birth to a girl and initiate a women's literary collective that morphs into a social justice arts organization. But unlike my parents, who encountered challenges when choosing to marry outside their communities, René and I receive only support from our respective families. Both sides of our families understand the challenges of splintered histories.

In May 2016, when René is offered work opportunity in Pasadena, California, we decide to try something new, especially since our daughter Minal will be entering middle school, a transition period for her. We visit Pasadena, rent a partly-furnished condominium, and register Minal in a public school similar to the one she attends in Houston.

Ten days prior to our departure, my mother, who I call Ammi and who has been moving between Houston, Boston (with my sister), and our Karachi home, returns to Houston to join my friends to help me pack or discard; René and I are shipping only two cubes to Pasadena. We are using our move as an opportunity to shed and are giving away most of our furniture before leaving Houston.

*

While my mother folds and packs my saris, bedcovers, carpets, and curtains—fabrics I've collected from Pakistan and India for more than 30 years—my friend Anita comes over to help me with my books.

Rolling up her sleeves, she pulls a hardcover off the bookshelf. "You want to keep this one?" she asks. "Tell me why."

"It's signed to me," I reply.

Though a writer herself, Anita responds by tearing out the signed page. "Make an art installation later," she says. Having recently moved from Cambridge, Massachusetts to Houston to be with her parents who were born in India, Anita understands the challenges of relocation. "If I want a book now," she tells me, "I go to the library."

Remembering the paperbacks that I shipped 30 years ago from South Hadley to Karachi only to recently give away, I am grateful for Anita's commitment to shed. At the end of our two-day session—even though I feel as my body is being slashed with a knife each time I make a choice to keep or discard a book—my stack is reduced from 25 boxes to 10.

A few days before we are to fly out of Houston's Hobby airport, I survey our baggage; my mother will drive to the airport with us and then fly east. Counting four suitcases, three pieces of hand baggage, and a cat, I decide to call Uber for an airport ride. I don't know anyone with a car big enough to fit us and our belongings.

But when my friend Oui hears my idea, she laughs. "*You*

can't take an Uber out of Houston!"

The morning of our departure, Oui arrives with her husband Albert. My friends Oskar and Lauren also join us. Cramming into two cars, we weave toward the airport. Once we unload, Oui, Albert and Oskar stay with us till we walk through the security checkpoints. As Ammi, Minal and I unpack Minal's cat, Nora, our laptops and our IPads, Oui, Albert and Oskar stand behind the roped line, waving to us. We wave back.

Ammi turns to me to say: "This feels like Karachi!"

Even after we complete security, collect our items and tie our shoelaces, Oskar, Oui and Albert remain at the roped line, keeping us in their line of vision as long as they can.

Once we take off, Minal sneaks her cat Nora out of her hamper, and the two gaze out of the airplane window at the sky scattered with grey and white clouds.

*

Reflecting on my mother's life trajectory, I recognize that I have followed her pattern of crossing borders, marrying outside my community, and leaving my childhood home with few objects (a badminton racquet, books, fabrics) and many memories. Ammi and I have flown, driven, and taken trains to depart from at least six cities to relocate across national and international borders, and she and I can no longer pin down a single geographical location that defines "home." However, no matter where she lands, Ammi creates community by teaching and cooking, while I initiate projects such as my arts organization, *Borderlines*, and *On Belonging* to process my geographic and cultural location. But Minal, who has spent many summers in Karachi and is fluent in Spanish, is only beginning to process her connection to three international borders, and her departure from the city in which she was born. In an essay about home, friendship, and belonging, for which she was awarded a 2017 National Scholastic prize, Minal uses writing and voice to grapple with her first move, stating that once she makes "long lasting friends, I can call Pasadena a home just as I do Houston."

This Ritual Is Mine

by CYNTHIA GUARDADO

from *ENDEAVOR*

There is something beautiful about this flower
damp like skin unfurled. Everything is blooming ruby
and here I bring jamaica back to life.
Its flower stretches across water,
its thirst greater than mine.
My palm drips, each flower still bleeding,
a fist full of ancestry. My great grandmothers

and my grandmothers
are huddled around a fire
over their brewing tea. I have it here
for another kind of survival—
my kidney's thirsty too. Jamaica, you're everywhere:
waving in the wind outside my window.
The power you carry is in our tradition and
scientists doubt you, they say you are not reliable,
they ask for evidence. But there is no way to prove

how you reach inside me, into my blood
and pull out the infection that eats away at me.
This is my meditation for you,
for all of your crimson love.
For my grandmother,
for all my great grandmothers,
for the women—the roots of my life.

In Another Life

by JANEL PINEDA

from *WILDNESS*

The war never happened but somehow you and I still exist. Like obsidian,
we know only the memory of lava and not the explosion that created

us. Forget the gunned-down church, the burning flesh, the cabbage soup.
There is no bus. There is no border. There is no blood. There are

only sweet corn fields and mango skins. The turquoise house and clotheslines.
A heaping plate of pasteles and curtido waiting to be disappeared into our bellies.

In this life, our people are not things of silences but whole worlds bursting
into breath. Everywhere, there are children. Playing, clothed and clean.

Mozote does not mean massacre and flowers bloom in every place shoes are
left behind. My name still means truth, this time in a language my mouth recognizes,

in a language I know how to speak. My grandmother is still a storyteller although I am
not a poet. In this life, I do not have to be. This poem somehow still exists. It is told

in my mother's voice and she makes hurt dissolve like honey in hot water, manzanilla
warming the throat. You and I do not find each other on another continent, grasping

at each other's necks in search of home. We meet in a mercado, my
arms overflowing
with mamey and anonas, and together we wash them in riverwater.
We watch sunset fall over

a land we call our own and do not fear its taking. I bite into the
fruit, mouth sucking
seed from substance, pulling its veins from between my teeth. Our
laughter echoes

from inside the cave, one we are free to step outside of. We do not
have to hide here.
We do not have to hide anywhere. A torogoz flies past my face and
I do not fear its flapping.

The Button Maker's House

by SAKAE MANNING

from *CARVE MAGAZINE*

The wind howled through the San Gabriel Mountains and pushed right up into every crack and crevice of the chilly old map maker's house. That's what neighbors called it. A dowry home built by a cartographer for his only daughter in the early 1900s. A house intended for a large family. One with loud, laughing children. Fort builders. Tree climbers. A family who loved doors and windows that could be slung open from all sides of the house. At the center of the front garden, a Deodar Cedar, taller than any tree for blocks around, broad branched, and regal, planted for shade, a children's swing, a place for family gatherings. The tree reminded Mari of the flat-topped cedars growing at the edge of her grandfather's village in Japan. Bending to the ocean's whims, shaped by monsoons and tsunamis, but never breaking. The four intertwined trunks created a perfect spot for marrying up to the big-nosed man Mari's mother believed held so much potential.

Mari rubbed her eyes, worrying about the bougainvillea, the roses, and even the Deodar in the early October windstorm. With every gust, thick planked doors rattled on old brass hinges. Undeterred, the wind moved upwards, through the big-boned attic, to the debris strewn back yard. It left the season's final persimmons, already shredded by wild parrots, in little festering heaps on the cold lawn. It wound its way up into the barn, causing the hanging lights above Mari's work area to sway. Magnifying glasses trembled on long metal arms bolted to a work table made from a knotty old door.

The wind growled before rushing on to the next street. Mari shivered, folded the hand drawn patterns, wrapped the deer bone she was tooling into handbag fasteners, and put everything inside her jacket pockets. *I should be used to this by now*, she thought, clicking the flashlight on and off, *It's October, and this is Southern California. The land of wind and fire.*

She shined the light on her hand, considered the six intricately carved wooden buttons hanging framed on one wall. After a quick glance, she decided they'd be safe, wrapped a woolen scarf around her neck, hugged her sketchbooks close, and turned off the lights. The flashlight bounced, a lost yellow ball, as Mari ran to the house. Her breathing quickened to keep the wind from whipping through her own drafty insides.

She burst through the back door and was greeted by the tall front windows shaking each time a fresh gust made its way across deserts, highways, gated communities, through valleys, dusting up deer trails. Mari felt the brewing wind, her neighbors' worry, and knew this time was different. Not like two years ago when the wind blew out a transformer in the middle of her baking a Thanksgiving turkey. Not like five years ago when the wind scattered neighbors' patio furniture, garden signs, and her own chimney cover onto cars and into neighbors' yards. That year, her husband joked, they weren't in Kansas anymore. Neighbors who never spoke beyond a polite nod, crossed expansive, manicured lawns, stepped carefully over flattened shrubbery, stood gripping steaming coffee mugs in the street, and assessed the damage. Then, there was ten years ago when the Santa Anas blew so hard, their front awning, an aluminum paneled add on, painted in green and white stripes, was left hanging by a nail. Her husband, ripped it down declaring he never liked the awning anyway. It didn't fit with the house. He left it twisted and jagged for Mari and Mr. Burris, their 75-year-old lawn man, to clean up.

It was Mr. Burris who had first warned Mari about the Santa Anas. "You'll see how much suffering happens when the town gets caught with its pants around its ankles," he said. He leaned his head towards Echo Mountain where The White Castle once stood. Molten iridescent glass fused to broken kitchen tile, and rusted, hand forged nails blanketed the resort's rocky foundation. "I rest my case," he'd said, snorting and twitching his nose with an exaggerated nod. Mari knew he was right. Twenty years living on the crooked street taught her the Santa Anas were as much a part of Altadena's history, its seasons of destruction, as Christmas Tree Lane or brown bears swimming in chlorinated pools.

This was the wind that dwelled in Death Valley's Great Basin, whispering and toiling until it found purpose. At first, the storm was long and breathy. Autumn leaves and pine needles fluttered down the lane into piles readied for bagging. In late afternoon, Mari felt it simmering; heard it whistling sharply up in the mountains. By dusk, its gaze turned to the rows of homes creeping up into the foothills. Power and county trucks rumbled up and down the mountain. Generators were pulled out of garages. Planters and lawn chairs stowed away. Squirrels burrowed down in their nests. Hummingbirds disappeared; their voices muted by the dry air. Crows and hawks hunkered under ragged stone ledges to avoid being blown away from the only mountains they'd ever known.

This was the wind that had burned down the town's beloved White Castle in 1906. Mr. Burris said the wealthy guests could see all the way to the Pacific Ocean from the resort perched on the mountain top. Mari looked up towards the ruins, wondered out-loud if the map maker's daughter planned to honeymoon on Echo Mountain. Mr. Burris followed Mari's eyes, squinted, "Louise was her name," twitched his nose, and chuckled, "now that's what old folks call a what- coulda-shoulda-woulda story, since Louise's betrothed died a few days before making it down from Frisco." Mari looked surprised. Mr. Burris held his hand up, "But folks said she was content—lived alone in the dowry home until she died a spinster."

*

The electricity shut off and on, even flickered brown, for hours now. Mari told her husband it was good to have a flashlight and to keep Ollie close. She slipped a sweater onto Ollie, while her husband watched. He picked up the flashlight Mari left on the nightstand, checked to make sure the batteries were good before tucking it in bed next to Ollie, who squeezed her chunky body between them, wagging a stubby tail. Mari pulled her hiking headlamp over a knitted cap. They wore sweats and t-shirts in case they had to run outside for a damage check; plus, the heat went out with the last power surge.

It wasn't long before her husband fell asleep, hand in his sweats, a laptop on his chest, wearing earbuds, porn pounding into his head. He'd always insisted it was music. Mari tried to see his side, but after twenty years dangling from a marriage with loose ends, she turned her head, shut her eyes, as women screaming "yes, give it to me hard, daddy," throbbed from his ears. She lifted herself up on an elbow, staring at her husband's sunburned nose. It was coated in aloe gel, pointed, not flat and wide like hers, had the curves and bumps found on marble busts in museums. Mari was surprised his eyes, cheeks, the area around his ears, were wrinkled, speckled in freckles and spots. *Why hadn't I noticed before?* An unsettling feeling rose in her. The kind she got when he didn't come home at night.

Mari lay awake listening to him and to Ollie snore. The small bedside lamp cast a dim, yellowish light, anchoring them to the room. She regretted leaving the framed wooden buttons, but it wasn't safe to go out now. She had spent years carving a honey bee, a lavender sprig, cedar cone, a bird's nest, rosebud, and a hummingbird onto the top of each round, good-sized button. "They're fine," she assured herself, listening to the wind getting louder as it reached their house and moaned through the giant Deodar in the front yard. Her husband wanted the tree cut down. "It's messy," he'd said. Mari tried to humor him, "It sheds its coat like an animal sheds hair, and besides," Mari explained reverently, "Mr. Burris says the Deodar Cedar is the tree of God." Her husband had grunted and kicked at the brown needles collecting at the trunk's base.

She distracted herself from thinking about the buttons by imagining her husband walking around the big roomed house with a white haze following him. Mari called it a chemical trail. It was bleach, which he used liberally when washing his underwear separately, not with towels, definitely not with her underwear. She shrugged, furrowed her brow, and imagined filling his plate with overcooked Americanized Chinese food he'd bring home, while he opened all the fortune cookies and read the tiny paper slips, bragging about his excellent luck.

Mari pressed her words against her teeth, forming a tight smile. Her husband found things on the street or left in hotel rooms, lucky things—cufflinks encrusted with his birthstones, expensive cologne in his favorite scent. He won every raffle—flat screen televisions, cell phones, a set of golf clubs. Lingering questions stuck more than a few times on her lips, but Mari wiped them away like crumbs from a stale cracker. She sat motionless through his outrageous stories and congratulated him on having good fortune. Luck is something you make for yourself he told her and pondered out-loud if Mari wasn't trying hard enough. Being a button maker isn't a very serious career he'd observed. Maybe she should dye the gray in her hair, wear make-up, get a real job. Mari doubted her husband and his luck, but tied a scarf over her hair anyway.

She studied his sleeping face. His eyelids flitting in some dream; probably resting on other women's faces, their asses. Tonight, the normally confusing lies she told herself were blown clear by the Santa Ana winds. She spoke a truth. Her husband liked any woman but her. He had a particular leaning towards Asian women who looked 16, small framed, smaller breasts. Mari knew this from the porn she'd caught glimpses of, ran her hand up and down her throat to keep from choking on an over feeding of denials and knew she couldn't change what should have been noticed all along. "Come on, Ollie," Mari slapped her thigh, and the dog jumped up, following

Mari to the kitchen. She couldn't stop worrying about the buttons. Mari turned on the outside lights with no luck. "Maybe the fuse is blown," she said, leaning her face into the oversized kitchen window, peering towards the barn. She could make out a bird bath lying on its side, but everything else fell away into blackness. An abyss stood between her and the six buttons.

*

Early on, they had decorated the Deodar together, wiring Christmas ornaments and lights to sturdy branches. Those were the years they tried to have children. She pictured the embryos struggling to set roots. After each loss, Mari carefully wrapped a few drops of the blood that came after in cheesecloth. She tooled and whittled a button, from a pattern traced around a tarnished Kennedy fifty cent piece. The wood chopped and seasoned after Mr. Burris trimmed a thick lower branch from the tree. Mari carved a secret compartment in each cedar button where she used needle-nosed tweezers to pack and seal a tiny shred of bloodied cloth inside.

Meanwhile, the Deodar, grew taller, wider, stronger, shading the entire front yard. The camellia bushes withered; the morning glories stopped blooming. Mr. Burris had said living things needed light to thrive. It was a choice. The tree or the things that grew around it. Mari chose the tree. The place she believed her love was affirmed, her worth set and valued, by a marrying up husband under the tree of God.

This past summer, Mr. Burris had said the drought was taking a toll on trees, weakening their roots. Mari relayed this news to her husband on a sweltering Sunday drive home from the hardware store, reminding him Mr. Burris was an expert, a retired botanist. She noted the disappearing oaks, pointed to the blocks left with sawdust filled sockets where trees once formed shady archways. Her husband tilted his head, glanced out the car window where she motioned, and asked, "Who is Mr. Burris again?" Mari lowered the car temperature, turned the vents towards her, and stared out her own window. By the time they unloaded the car, he had forgotten about the Santa Anas. He was never concerned about the things that mattered, and Mari knew it would catch up with them one day.

Mari returned to bed, letting Ollie jump up first. She chewed on her lip, cracked her knuckles, and was soon thinking about the deer bone clasps. She pulled out her sketchbook and looked down at her husband, snoring, air whistling in and out of his mouth, winding its way around the high ceiling. The wind churned, lifting the house in stops and starts. Mari heard it swimming in circles up into the walls and knew there would be a fine silt coating the window ledges inside her kitchen, the bath, her barn studio. She sketched in short, quick strokes, thinking of her mother. She'd advised Mari marrying a light haired man, a lawyer from Santa Monica, was going to improve her life; the life of her unborn children. Her mother, eyes weary from explaining, pursed her lips, "It's called 'marrying up,'" and shook her head sadly, "Everyone knows it's important, Mariko." She tapped her temple three times, looking into Mari's eyes, "Everyone but you." She'd told Mari these things in Japanese, so her father couldn't understand. "I thought we would be forever," Mari whispered, leaning close to her husband's ear, her throat parched. Her husband shuddered in his sleep, a humping, huffing, shrieking ear bud fell loose around his neck. She wound the earbuds around her fingers, shut the computer, and slid it under the bed.

The house creaked, the walls closed in tighter, readying itself for the hardest winds yet to come. The neighbor's trash cans stopped rolling in the driveway outside. Her husband's snoring became the only noise in the house. She smoothed his hair back and noticed thinning towards the top. She rested her hand on Ollie's belly; could feel her sleeping soundly. Big, scary Ollie, a pit- bull mix who found Mari up on Chaney Trail, bony, ticks peppering her underbelly, a bloated deer tick hanging from a swollen eye lid, a choke chain grown into her neck. A silver-coated dog that suddenly appeared from a grove of trees, as if she had been waiting for Mari. The vet postulated Ollie had found her way out of hell to the mountains. The mountains brought her to Mari, because dogs know who they want. He said they have good instincts, scratched Ollie's ears, while handing Mari Ollie's leash. She kept Ollie even though her husband complained about the vet bills, an increase in homeowner's insurance, and had questioned where the dog would sleep. "It has worms for God's sake," he'd groaned. "Mari," his voice rising and deepening, eyes darkening, "Mariko, are you listening to me?"

The electricity hummed. The power lines buzzed and snapped, leaving the map maker's house in darkness.

Mr. Burris had understood her love for the Cedar but it was choking the lemon trees; the storm gutters were filled with needles. He pushed his large brimmed straw hat back to wipe his brow, drank the ice water she offered. They'd sat under the Deodar for the rest of that afternoon sharing Mr. Burris' lunch, a Hershey's bar from Webster's, and her husband's beer. Mr. Burris had helped start the local Black History Month parade. He's proud it's now a tradition. "Just like these Italian bambinos," he patted the tree's dense trunk. His voice boomed with pride, "Cedrus Deodara, the tree of God, from the Himalayas, to Italy, across the sea to America." He told Mari how the seeds came in a horse drawn wagon on dirt roads before being carefully planted and grown into saplings. "Laborers planted them" he'd said absentmindedly flicking dried grass from his shirt. "Chinese fellas," he lifted his eyebrows, looked at Mari. "I'm Japanese," she reminded him. "Yes, that's right," Mr. Burris laughed. He speculated on how a Deodar got into her yard when most of the old ones grew on Santa Rosa Avenue. "I'm of the belief," he once said, "those Chinese fellas took a few of those saplings and planted them for folks on the side." He had winked, made a boxer's fist, and told her the trunks winding around and clinging to each other was a sign of determination. He had the smile of a kind man, a man who spoke truth, didn't ask too many questions.

Maybe, Mr. Burris had speculated, Louise loved the tree in place of the family she never had. He offered Mari a wooden toothpick from his shirt pocket, scraping a thumbnail over the lemon clutched in his free hand. He asked Mari what she thought about that. She tapped the toothpick between her teeth, leaned her head back, imagined Louise on the bench where they were now sitting, and said, "It's an easy tree to love." Mr. Burris flicked his toothpick up and down on his bottom lip for some time. The silence set his words in Mari's mind. The toothpick shifted to dangling from the corner of his mouth.

*

The wind wrapped this memory up in a surge of air, swallowing the sky and pulled the two-hundred-year-old Deodar harder. Rebellious and unrelenting, the wind wheezed and cleared its throat, spitting on the entire town. The Italian Deodar swatted the roofline, the side of the house. The Santa Anas roared and whipped, catching in the window screens, ripping picket fences apart, and billowing car covers. Mari heard the old tree crack, loud like thunder rolling through the wide-mouthed valley after a brilliant lightning burst. They hurriedly slipped on sneakers, made their way outside, pointing the flashlight into blackness. A massive shadow heaving, as high as roiling ocean wave, breaking in the wind, was all they could make out. The flailing branches pulling away, while the wind stubbornly pushed them down.

The tree didn't know it had already lost. The ancient Santa Anas knew the land it traversed, and the tree, no matter if it was God's tree, wasn't of this place. The Deodar became its own forest, drowning the entire side of the house, enveloping their bedroom, the windows, the original oiled staircase. It rested on the map maker's house, for it had not been this close to the ground for over a hundred years. They could hear the roof heaving. Its final attempt to resist under the weight of the Cedar overwhelmed by lunging tree branches. Glass shattered. Pipes burst. Ollie barked. Mari and her husband watched. Another crack, louder than the first, echoed, leaving Mari's ears numb. The Deodar relented. The lemon trees and camellia bushes planted by the map makers daughter, even the wrought iron fence, were lost.

As sudden as it left, the wind shifted back towards the map maker's house. Mari's husband stood there, legs wide, flashlight in one hand, lemons in the other, his sweats, a threadbare Bob Marley tee, and open jacket flapping against his paunch in the wind. He was wearing a ski hat. She was surprised. After twenty years of constantly warning him to protect his head from the cold, he finally listened. He was angry at the fallen tree and yelled at the wind. The words galloped away from Mari. She stared at her husband, trying to read his lips between the flickering flashlight and half shadows. She leaned over to study the roots and soil pulled clean out of the ground and thought of the entrails from a cat she once saw gutted, left on a driveway by coyotes. The fresh scent of cedar torn, its damp insides not meant for such a violent end, filled Mari's entire body, raised memories of her lost children, the wooden buttons hanging in her studio.

"Insurance," he yelled. "Fucking," his words stabbed at the wind. "Damn tree," weaved over to her.

Mari let the wind carry her, nearly on tiptoes, into the house. It was dark, smelled of the garden after a long day's rain. The headlamp illuminated Mari's search. She found her pack in the entry closet, a sleeping bag still attached from her last trip into the mountains, shook the water bladder. It was full. The dining room chandelier was hanging awkwardly by a wire, the china cabinet had fallen across the polished dining room table. The wind whistled through the open ceiling. She could see stars through parts of the attic. Debris—leaves, a bird's nest, dirt—skittered, falling over the rooms. Water gurgled from ruptured pipes, flooding the upstairs bedrooms. Mari looked around, the headlamp shining on each broken part of the map maker's house. *Louise's dowry home*, Mari thought, trembling, and stepped carefully around the splintered table to dig through clean laundry on the back porch. She bundled underwear, socks, a pair of hiking pants hanging on the rack, and stuffed everything into the pack. She slipped on woolen socks found tucked into her hiking boots, laced them up, and called for Ollie. She filled a large plastic bag with kibble, called for Ollie again. "Scary little pitty," Mari cooed out-loud, "Where are you?" Mari found Ollie cowering behind the coffee table, still wearing the sweater, soothed, and leashed her.

They maneuvered around water dripping from the ceiling to the kitchen door and stepped outside into the full force of the Santa Anas. The headlamp shined on the barn's wide roofline, and marked their path to the studio's side door. They ran, sidestepping, sometimes leaping, over fallen peppercorn tree branches and broken flower pots. She looked to the wall where the buttons hung, but they were gone. Mari's heart skipped before she pointed her headlamp to the floor and saw the shattered frame. The buttons already covered in silt. She wiped each one on her sleeve before hastily dropping them into her pack and running back to the front lawn.

She didn't look at her husband, standing near the tree, yelling against the wind. He missed her folding a trail map, sliding it into her jacket pocket, walking up the street, turning right at the corner onto Lake Avenue, towards the trailhead. The sky was swelling, going from early morning graphite to a full rusty haze, as the sun came around Mt. Wilson. *There must be a fire somewhere*, she sniffed, focusing her gaze on the farthest point north. She wrinkled her brow, the way she did at the market when she couldn't recall the final thing needed for a recipe. Her thumb tapped her ring finger. Her wedding band was on the nightstand, now crushed along with the bed, her books, and her husband's laptop. She pulled the winter cap down closer, over her ears. The smoke was faint. She looked beyond the San Gabriel's, trees rising and leaning in concert with the wind in a cloudless sky.

Half a block uphill, a large oak had fallen across a Honda, and in its final descent, the tree branches became caught up in swinging power lines, pulling them down as easily as tearing a loose four-holed button from a pair of weathered trousers. The pole, weakened by woodpeckers and beetles, snapped, lay jagged and useless. Mari walked onto the porch, where a man in his 80's stood, rocking back and forth in a faded plaid robe and bare feet, suggested he get dressed and put on a hat. Shiny headed with wispy hair above his ears, he reminded her of the final wildflower patches at summer's end. She smelled old coffee, imagined milk already cooling on the kitchen counter, and by day's end, it would sour from lack of refrigeration. Mari wondered if he had a flashlight or candles, someone to call for help. These questions ran through her head, but she asked nothing. Only nodded, touched his bony elbow, and smiled, "I've got to push on." He patted Ollie on her hind quarters, asked where she lived, and Mari replied, "the map maker's house." She raised her chin slightly, "but you can call it the button maker's house," and laughed louder and deeper than she could ever remember doing. The wispy haired man chuckled. Mari looked at Ollie and made a clicking sound in her cheek, causing the dog to wiggle and prance.

They trudged, against the wind, admiring the fierce Santa Anas. Palm fronds flitted down the road past her, a dotting of trash cans lay jammed against the curb and more along a chain link fence. She kept walking, past the next long block, the leaves dancing before falling at her feet, past the park baseball field, the parking lot littered with food wrappers, a couple of baseballs rolling around, the community building. She felt the wind inside her now, shifting and filling the drafty spaces in her heart, her lungs, beckoning her to the mountains. Ollie trotted alongside, ears up, eyes narrowed. Mari felt as if they were gliding towards the trailhead. Just ahead. Empty. A small funnel of debris spiraling up from the worn path, and licked her lips, anticipating all the meandering trails leading deep into the mountains. She stepped onto the trail. A wall of cacti and rock on her left; the canyon falling to her right, pausing. The wind tapped at her back. "Trust the Santa Anas, Ollie," Mari said. She'll take us to where the wind lives."

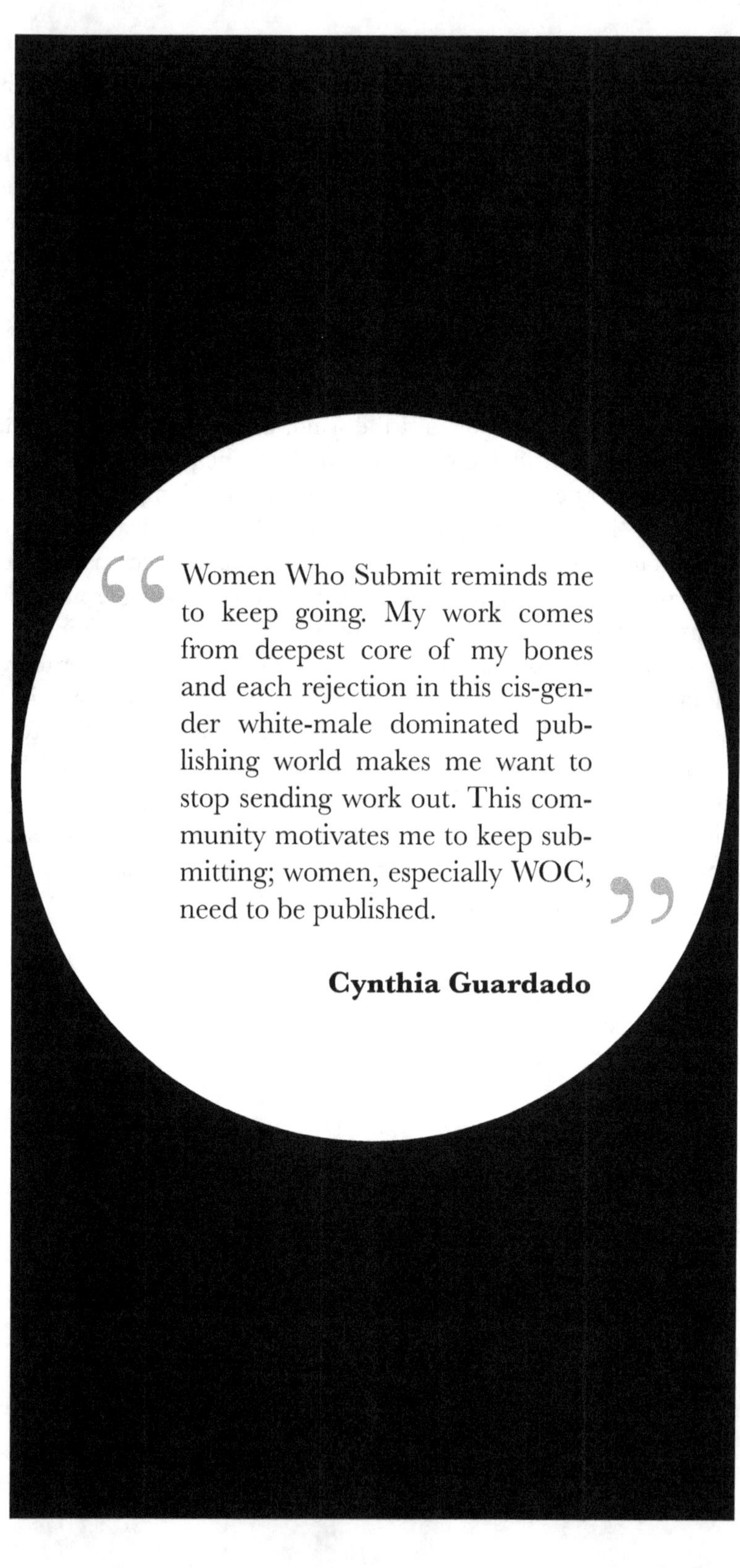
"Women Who Submit reminds me to keep going. My work comes from deepest core of my bones and each rejection in this cis-gender white-male dominated publishing world makes me want to stop sending work out. This community motivates me to keep submitting; women, especially WOC, need to be published."
Cynthia Guardado

Mother

by ARIELLE SILVER

from *MATADOR REVIEW*

Mother: [Noun] a woman who has borne a child.

1. First came love.

Father: Spring break she took a road trip down from Georgia for the weekend. Ended up at my frat party.

Where are you from? I asked.
New York, she said.
Your name sounds Jewish, I said.
I am, she said.
What's that on your finger? I asked.
I'm engaged, she said.
Why don't you break up with your fiancé and go out with me, I said.

2. Then came marriage.

Father: About a month or so later she called to say they broke up, so I caught a Greyhound to Valdosta. She drove me back to the bus on Sunday; I proposed.

Sure, she said.

Never took her eyes from the road. We married in August. Well, the chapel had already been arranged, the dress, the menu.

a. As planned:
   i. Chapel
   ii. Rabbi
   iii. Family of the bride

iv. Dress

b. Plan modified:
i. Groom
ii. Groom's family

The Holmes-Rahe Stress Inventory lists marriage as seventh most stressful of life events.

---

3. Then came baby.

Mother: [Noun] the female parent of a plant or animal

4. Mother became a parent
    a. 17 months after the wedding (respectable)
    b. 5:35 a.m. (a week late)
    c. in a hospital (in Florida)
    d. to a daughter.

5. Pregnancies (1975-1980):
    a. First: born (daughter)
    b. Second: aborted
    c. Third: miscarried
    d. Fourth: born (son)

The Holmes-Rahe Stress Inventory lists pregnancy as twelfth most stressful of life events.

Mother: [Noun] the origin or source of something

The Holmes-Rahe Stress Inventory lists gaining a new family member as fourteenth most stressful of life events.

But:

6. moving cannot be dismissed (four homes, three states in three years)

because:

---

the Holmes-Rahe Stress Inventory lists
major change in living condition (new
home, remodeling, deterioration of
neighborhood or home etc.) as
twenty-eighth,

---

and

---

changing to a new school as thirty-third

---

7. [Daughter
    a. Grade 1 (FL)
    b. Grade 2 (NY)
    c. Grade 3 (NJ)]

---

and changes in residence as thirty-second

(see above),

and

---

major change in the health or behavior
of a family member as eleventh most
stressful of life events,

---

8. and Mother's behavior did seem to change

Father: Perhaps it was hormones. She wasn't like that when we met.

Mother: [Transitive verb] to look after or care for as a mother does

---

but also, the Holmes-RaheStress
Inventory lists spouse beginning or
ceasing work outside the home as
twenty-sixth

---

and changing to a different line of work as
eighteenth most stressful of life events,

---

9. Mother did want a career

a. Lost dreams, known:
i. Archeologist
ii. Fashion Designer

b. Careers, known:
i. Hebrew school teacher
ii. Avon lady
iii. Market researcher
iv. Museum administrator
v. Caterer
vi. Hebrew school principal

10. and Daughter could babysit Son:
a. House key pinned in school bag.
b. 4:45 pm: Son's baby cheeks wet with tears. Son stood in garage fretful with stomach-eating anxiety. Son wanted Mother.
c. 4:45 pm: Daughter drank SlimFast from the cabinet and ate two bowls of Chex.

---

the Holmes-Rahe Stress Inventory lists major change of responsibilities as twenty-second most stressful of life events,

---

d. and watched reruns of *Three's Company*, *Happy Days*, and *Laverne and Shirley* until *Different Strokes* and *The Facts of Life* came on,
e. folded laundry,
f. ran fingers through the carpet until garage door opened. Mother arrived. Crying stopped.

Mother: [Transitive verb] something regarded as the biggest, most impressive, or most important; example: the mother of all yard sales

11. Mother's beauty:

She is *so* pretty! said the Teachers, Sales Clerks, Librarians

a. Beauty items:

i. nail polish
ii. shaving razors
iii. eye shadow
iv. tweezers

b. Fitness:
i. "20-minute Workout"
ii. Jogs

c. Diet:
i. SlimFast
ii. Weight Watchers

12. Daughter's beauty:

Am I pretty? Daughter asked.
I wouldn't say pretty, said Mother. *I'd say striking. But your belly sticks out. Try sit-ups. And vertical wall slides. Your bottom sticks out.*

Mother: [Adjective] derived or learned from or as if from one's mother; native

13. Daughter: *I will not let chocolate pass these lips*

14. Afterschool, revised:
a. SlimFast
b. No Chex

15. Not permitted (for Daughter):
a. nail polish
b. shaving razors
c. eye shadow
d. tweezers
e. haircuts

f. Converse (*Your feet are too long*)
g. Boots (*You'll grow out of them*)
h. Jeans (*When you're older*)
i. Logos (*You don't want to be a walking advertisement.*)

The Holmes-Rahe Stress Inventory lists revision of personal habits (dress manners, associations, quitting smoking) as twenty-ninth most stressful of life events

---

16. Items taken:
    a. On the bathroom shelf: copper nail polish
    b. CVS: an eyeliner pencil.
    c. kitchen drawer: scissors (for legs, in lieu of a razor)

17. Mother: *She yanked out all her eyelashes!* [laugh, laugh, laugh]

18. Mother: *She tweezes her eyebrows!* [laugh, laugh, laugh]

Mother: [Noun] a woman having the responsibility and authority of a mother

19. Rules:
    a. Separate dishes: meat and dairy.
    b. No school on Jewish holidays.
    c. No trick-or-treating. (*Halloween is Pagan!*)
    d. No night time parties. (*There might be drinking!*)
    e. No entering a church. (*It's a sin!*)
    f. No concerts.
    g. No driving with friends. (*Cars are killing machines!*)
    h. No pins in the walls. (*We may sell this house!*)
    i. No dating (*Anyone, especially*:
        1. non-Jews
        2. black boys*
        3. girls**

        * Regardless of religion
        ** Obviously)

20. Family vacations:

    Mother: *Go without me*

    Daughter and Son: *Get a divorce already!*

The Holmes-Rahe Stress Inventory lists vacation as forty-first most stressful of life events.

Mother: [Slang] short for motherfucker, somewhat vulgar.

21. Holes in the bedroom doors
    a. Punched by Son:
        i. Attention needy?
        ii. Frustrated?
        iii. Lonely?
        iv. Anxious?

    b. Holes punched by Daughter:
        i. Frustrated, followed by hasty exits with:
            1. tooth-brush
            2. diary
            3. pens
            4. stuffed unicorn
            5. clarinet

The Holmes-Rahe Stress Inventory lists son or daughter leaving home (marriage, attending college, joined military) as twenty-third most stressful of life events.

---

22. First year of college, winter vacation:

Get out, Mother said,

and pulled the Volvo to the shoulder. Daughter got out. Mother drove off. South Florida summer heat, an unknown road, an unknown town; Daughter walked the white stripe.

Man in a pick-up truck, man in a semi, man in a Honda, man in a Mitsubishi: *Hey sweetie want a ride?*

Teeth clenched. Eyes to the white stripe. One hour. Two. White-painted combat boots; the asphalt white stripe.

Man like a dad in a Lexus: *Want a ride?*

Three days later, Mother returned.

Mother: [Verb] be or act as a mother; mothered, mothering

Mother: This is revisionist history. You have a terrible memory, just like your father.

You were not an affectionate child. You didn't like hugs.

You are my brilliant, beautiful, talented Daughter.

You should call more often. I miss you.

The Sound

by KATE MARUYAMA

from *WHISTLING SHADE*

Christine set the alarm for 4:30 a.m. on the day before Christmas Eve, 1961. She knew nothing could wake Chuck on a Saturday, but she fed him macaroni and cheese and wine the night before just in case. Not red wine, that gives him headaches. White. When Chuck drank, he always lit up bright red. He was a sagging, beardless version of Santa Claus when he finally stumbled off to bed.

She had been working on the cards to the children for a few weeks now. First in a notebook in her night table drawer. She thought really hard about each note. A few ideas that didn't sound right, she scribbled out. A few she added. When she thought they were ready, that she had said the most important things she needed to impart, she wrote each note onto a card. They were her grandmother's cards from the 1940s. She had been saving them because they were too nice to write on, just as her grandmother had saved them for the same reason. Small and rectangular, a spray of pine needles in one corner and a simple candle embossed with a golden flame. It was the kind of card they don't make anymore, but there'd be no point in saving them now.

To Sadie, 16, she wrote, "I love you. Be kind to your baby brother, he's going to grow up into a great guy. And remember—a boy will only go as far as you let him. Love, Mom."

To James, 14, she wrote, "I love you. Be patient with your father, he loves you so. Treat every girl like you would your sister. Love, Mom."

Charles, 18, was the hardest. She saved writing his until the middle of the morning, when the children were at school, Chuck was at work and there was no chance of interruption. In case she cried. So she'd have time to recover before she saw anyone. Charles was her oldest. "You were the first. Remember that. I loved when we used to sit and paint. I'm sorry things got hard. Remember, there is nothing you can't do in this world. I love you my little man grown big. Mom." Charles's was the only card she put in a sealed envelope. She had punched a hole in the corner of each and strung a ribbon through them the day before so that she could attach them to the presents more easily.

She woke up two minutes before the alarm went off. She turned it off, eased her covers back and slipped out of bed. Despite the cold, she didn't put on her slippers, for fear they would make noise. She pulled open the door and slipped through, looking back at the sleeping form of her husband. His shoulders were stacked sideways, rising and falling in the cool, blurry light of the streetlamp shining through the rain-rippled window. She could have picked a nicer morning for it, but here she was.

The night before, she had put her clothes for this morning in the guest bedroom. Now she cautiously avoided the squeakiest board in the hallway and slipped into the room, closing the door gently behind her. She slipped out of her robe and put on her stockings, her girdle and her slip. She could still fit in her pale green serge suit, but only with some work. The last button was a squeeze. She put on her brand new pink neoprene coat. It was amazing what they could do with fabrics these days. It was thickly woven and looked like wool, but was smoother when you touched it, made of some petrochemical substance that could keep the wind out better than wool. It was a brilliant pink, a Jackie Kennedy sort of pink with a matching pillbox hat. Christine loved this coat, and bought pink alligator pumps and a matching purse to go with. She put on her coat and slipped the cards out of the drawer of a side table where she'd stashed them two days before. She carried her shoes and handbag downstairs.

The Christmas tree was still lit from the night before. Chuck had been too drunk, and she had been too preoccupied to turn it off. She was grateful now for the light it shed. She easily found the gifts and tied a card to each. A new dress from Rhodes for Sadie. A man-sized baseball glove for James. And for Charles, her journals. From before the war ended. From before Chuck stopped speaking to her. From before her life moved into a place she couldn't find herself in, or find her way out of.

She slipped out the kitchen door, so she wouldn't have to deal with the squeak from the front storm door hinge. The night before, she made up an excuse to leave her car in the driveway, put Chuck's in the garage: early Christmas errand, cream for the pie.

Everything was making extra noise this morning. The rain smattered on the car and bubbled down into the storm drain, the leafless tree branches clattered with a sudden gust of wind. Her breath rushed in her ears, her pink pumps scraped on the sidewalk. The shoes were completely wrong for the season, but that hadn't been part of her wardrobe calculations. Galoshes wouldn't be suitable. If nothing else, she would be put together. And in her pink neoprene coat with matching pumps and purse, damned if she weren't put together.

The first Vashon ferry ran at 5:30 that morning. The man in the ticket booth took her fare and looked her over, "Where you going, looking so pretty on a day like this?"

She smiled, nicely, putting her hand to her hair under her hat. "Oh, thank you. Nowhere special. But thank you." She pulled up to the waiting lanes and found she was first in line because of the holiday.

Christine met Chuck in 1940. There was a dance at the church and that man could cut a rug. He looked so handsome, green eyed and flushed in his brown suit and white shirt. The black tie, the well-cut hair and broad shoulders. His smile made him look like someone who would take care of you. They exchanged a few pleasantries about the weather, fox-trotted to "Little Brown Jug" and it was agreed that he would meet her at the dance at the community center the following week. So their relationship progressed from dance to dance, small talk, a quick kiss in the back hall by the ladies' room, a grope in the car. When the location of their dates left the dance hall for local restaurants, Chuck made decisions for her, when they would meet, where they would go, what they would order. Having practically raised her sisters since her mother died, Christine decided that it felt good to be taken care of. Someone else could make the decisions for a while.

They were married in 1940. She had Charles and Sadie during the war. James came soon after. Chuck went off to serve in the Officers' Corps in Biloxi, pushing boots. It seemed like every time he came home on leave, Christine would come down pregnant. She liked those years, rambling around with the children, taking care of the local widows, starting women's groups. She and the girls pooled their babysitting hours and she became a part-time secretary at Boeing.

Each day stretched before her with choices and purpose and reason. From planting victory gardens, to figuring out what meal to cook from the rations allowed, to organizing the children in her charge for that day. When it was her day to babysit, she and seven children (two families and her own two) would sing, play, bake cookies, and, best of all, paint. She lined up miniature easels made from wood scraps from Boeing in the back yard. She put out tempera paints in used tin cans. The rule at Christine's house was there were no limits on the amount of paint you could use.

When she was at work, she was in charge of her boss's office, his comings and goings and meetings. Boeing was designing planes for the war and the control of information within the plant was imperative. Christine knew she was working for a higher cause.

She didn't know until Chuck came home for good in 1945, that what she'd really enjoyed about those years was freedom.

Chuck brought his officers' military precision home with him. She thought at first that he was having trouble adjusting to the post-war period. Or that she was having trouble adjusting to someone else helping run the house. They were little things at first, particularities about where to leave his shirts, how to put away the dishes. She was understanding when he made her quit her job to better tend to things around the homestead. She was in the same boat as her girlfriends from Boeing. Used to riveting planes and fixing their own cars, they were sent back to the trenches of hand-washed laundry, cooking and cleaning. Days ran one into the other with no company but their children.

She kept her Tuesday night women's bowling team and there they could express their frustration together. They laughed about old times in the work force, bowled, talked a little about their husbands, sighed wistfully and went home to their respective lives.

Chuck's demands about shirts soon became demands about dinner, about how she spoke to the children. She swallowed her objections and forged forward. He had demands in the bedroom about which he no longer consulted her. There was a permission Chuck used to seek which he no longer felt necessary. Christine didn't think it was her place to fight it, but she missed the asking.

Life had called upon her and Christine figured she might as well rise to the occasion. Poor Betty Cooper's husband had been at Guadalcanal and some days couldn't leave the house for his shaking. She could be considerate, too.

But Chuck had only been as far as Biloxi.

He was good to the children. Christine stopped going to bowling nights because of Chuck's gruff sighs when she asked him if he would look after the children. She made one excuse and another with the girls until they just stopped asking. She lost that easy confidence found in community. Chuck seemed to know the most about the War, the Nazis, and now the Communists. His opinion on the price of food was penultimate, as were his opinions of the house, the meals, the children, the president and the latest automobile.

By the time James went off to Kindergarten, Christine realized that she had pleased and worked and changed and catered to Chuck's needs so much she had erased herself. She felt like she should fight back somehow before she disappeared entirely, but she no longer had the strength or dialogue with which to do it.

Nine years passed in this way. As the children grew into teenagers, with their own friends and their own schedules, Christine didn't know if she missed their needing her or if she was relieved that they were old enough to take care of themselves. Her responsibility for their moment to moment happiness had dissipated. It felt like a weight lifted. But in its place, unease had settled.

Then she got pregnant. She had loved carrying her three children, the feeling that she was doing something useful, purposeful in the world. But this pegnancy felt different from its beginning. At 38, she was so much older. She was sick not only in the morning, but all day and into the evening. She had a daily, hour to hour alarmingly ground-dropping sense of fear and dread that would overtake her so swiftly at times that she would have to sit down suddenly to gather herself. Whatever she did to ward it off, baking, cleaning, sewing, a sense of despair grew in her, a loudening rhythmic thud.

She was getting her courage together to tell Chuck about the pregnancy, when he made a crack about the "eyetalian" family down the street and their five kids. Something racist and then something about old ladies and shoes. Unable to face his disapproval, Christine claimed that she was ill in those weeks leading up to Christmas and took to her bed. The children didn't seem to mind. They'd check in on her and get their own dinner. She listened to the voices of her family at dinnertime in the kitchen below, talking, sometimes laughing.

One day, feeling a little better, Christine went out Christmas shopping. She picked up the dress and the baseball mitt. She stopped in front of the local church to make sure she hadn't left her car keys at the store. As she fished in her pocketbook, she looked up to see the manger scene out front on the brown, dead grass. There was straw strewn inside a rough wooden stable, a plaster Mary and Joseph, one shepherd, a sheep and a donkey. It was a quiet street, the hollow sound of the city echoed from a few blocks away, in another dimension. The manger lay empty, waiting for baby Jesus. It was a plaster manger, with fake molded straw painted on the sides. The center was a hollowed out dirty white that would later be covered with the baby and, presumably, real straw. But now, dully reflected the cold blue winter air, the gray-white baby-shaped pit revealed that the entire scene was a fraud. The plaster rippled where it had been poured and painted and where, year after year, it had gathered the city grime.

The vacant cavity hit her with a wave of nausea and emptiness that she hadn't felt before. There was no paint allowed there, no hay, no color, no curtains, no job, no opinions, no friends and no baby.

This child couldn't happen. The knowledge filled her with shame and dread. She wasn't fit for her family. She had become a void, a negative, a dark space that would need to remove itself.

*

Seattle was usually cold, but this unusually seeping bone-chilling irrecoverable cold started in December of that year. November was bleak, rain almost every day. But today's rain held that nose-pinching cold. Christine knew it would turn to ice and then probably snow by that night.

She would ditch the car in Port Angeles. She didn't want to hold people up by leaving an untended car on the ferry. Despite the warmth of her coat, the cold pricked her nose and her eyes stung. She breathed deeply, trying to focus. She was safely out of the house and on schedule.

The ferry was on time, the Klickitat. This was the same ferry she and the kids had ridden to pick strawberries on Whidbey Island last summer. A beautiful day, it should have been full of joy, but as she watched her beautiful girl and handsome boys stoop to pick up strawberries, laughter and freedom in their eyes, she knew that she was only watching life these days. She had put herself away with the paints years before.

The smell of exhaust filled the air and the swiftly approaching ferry churned its engines backwards to slow its advance. The water swirled and roared and as the boat docked, it squeaked against the pylons. A loud squeak one way, then another. Christine pulled at her gloves to straighten them, clicked shut her purse, left open from the ticket purchase. She patted her hair, straightened her hat and drove onto the ferry. There were only a few people getting onboard with her and two trucks. Early morning workers. Hell of a commute.

Christine parked her car and walked up the stairs to the upper deck, through the warmth and smell of coffee. The woman at the concession stand said, "Good morning." Christine nodded to her and tried to get away quickly. The woman called after her, "Merry Christmas!" But Christine didn't want any more human interaction. Or comfort. Or Danish. She stepped out back into the cold again. She couldn't do it here. The ferry ride was too short.

*

Two ferry rides and a short drive later, she drove up the Olympic Peninsula, the highway gently winding and mercifully empty. The sun wasn't up yet, but the sky was turning gray. After her anxiousness over the arrangements, she felt a peace come over her. It verged on elation. She had a plan and each step was going seamlessly.

*

An hour and a half later the ferry heaved out of Port Angeles. This was the route to Victoria. It was a long ride, and sleepier than the Puget Sound ferries. Christine watched from the upper deck as the bustle and tension of the shorter rides dissipated. After Friday Harbor, the crew relaxed, left the decks. Christine waited for the last of the passengers to leave their cars, or to relax into the rhythm of the ride. She clutched her purse, her hands numb from standing outside and walked back through the main cabin, through a metal door and down the narrow stairwell, her pumps clanking on the metal staircase. The engines had calmed from their starting-up churns, the sounds of the seagulls had thinned and she was alone, behind the chain, looking out as they passed Orcas island and into the open Pacific. It was cold here. She would sink. No one would have to deal with a body.

She looked behind her and saw a deckhand popping into a doorway. Now was the time. As she stepped over the chain, she caught a glimpse of her shoes. Those beautiful pink alligator shoes. She didn't want to lose her footing. She slipped them off and her stockinged foot stung with cold as it touched the metal deck. She put her purse down next to her shoes. Maybe someone would find them useful. Her personal information in the purse would allow the authorities to alert her family, so they wouldn't have to waste time searching for her. She wouldn't want them to think she'd run off on them. She said a prayer for God to take care of her children and she jumped.

Over and over she had imagined how it would go. The cold waves would close over her head, the intense cold would hit her and then she would begin to feel nothingness around her feet, which would spread to the rest of her body. Or, if she were lucky, she would fall unconscious instantly. She would fall beneath the waves, among the whales and, as the air left her lungs she would sink, gently, quietly silently to the bottom. Drowning was supposed to be very hard, but the cold was meant speed the process.

She felt the water later than she thought she would. Right after she jumped, she heard someone say, "Wait." She had imagined going feet first, but she somehow swiveled in the air and hit the water with her back. It hurt. When she hit the water, she realized that she was the one who had spoken.

The waves will close over her head. She waited for it. She went under, but only for a moment. Her head came up. She wasn't sinking. The boat was getting farther away and her hands and legs burned with the cold. Sharp pain started in her ankles and toes, but she wasn't sinking. Her coat. Her neoprene coat. It was acting like some sort of stylish pink floatation device. She had to get it off.

Cursing, she tried to bring her hands in to feel for her buttons. She grasped at one, but it bit her finger with the pain of contact. She tried harder, but she couldn't get purchase. The current had turned her back on the boat, which was by now, surely, out of site. She was staring at the shore of Orcas island. The sun was now up and bright and the world was unnaturally sharp and clear. The tall forest of pine trees on the shore of Orcas lined the cliffs. Some trees clung precariously, their roots and limbs reaching outward over the beach to where their fallen comrades lay, washed ashore from a passing logging boat. The sky was a perfect cerulean blue—Christine's favorite color in the paint box, that never got quite dark enough when she applied it to paper. As a child she was scolded for squirting an entire tube of watercolor onto one painting, but she had been working toward that blue sky.

From the ferry, the ocean past Orcas had looked so calm, but, bobbing in these two-foot waves and being pulled by the current, she knew it wasn't. Despite the violence of the motion, the water was so quiet, its only sound wet and rippling. The pain in her hands was subsiding. She started feeling sleepy. It may not be how she planned it, but surely she was giving in to hypothermia. She couldn't do much about the floating, but the effect would be the same.

She would sleep, it would be comfortable. Chuck would take care of the kids. Charles was going to college in the fall and James and Sadie could already take care of themselves. All of the worry and stress began to leave her and she felt at peace with wherever she was going. She felt happier than she'd been in awhile. As happy as after that first day of work at the plant. She should have known then, life was better, less complicated without Chuck. She thought his life would be better, less complicated, without her. Certainly the kids' lives. She began to feel dizzy and closed her eyes imagining swinging high under a maple tree. Her father had made her a wooden swing and when he hung it from their front tree she marveled at how such a simple thing could evoke such wonder. She swung forward and back, forward and back and there was a rumble. She thought *not with a bang but a rumble…*

All went black.

*

Everything hurt. She opened her eyes. Her head pulsated with a rhythmic thud, her skin burned, her feet had an internal ache like her bones were on fire. She found herself wrapped in a blanket in the interior of the ferry, right by the concession stand. Someone was trying to get her to drink some coffee. It spilled on her chin where it burned. She turned her head away. The first thing she felt was embarrassment. Someone had taken off her coat, she was down to her underthings and one of the deck hands was barking orders to a cluster of people who milled around her looking not worried, but afraid.

The deck hand had a broad, craggy face. The left side of his face was scarred, probably from the war. His skin was ruddy, flushed, making the rippled scar shine white. Maybe it was shrapnel. Or some sort of burn. *It burns.*

He said, "You gave us quite a scare there, lady. If we hadn'ta found your purse and your shoes, well…I don't want to think what woulda happened."

She said, "I'm sorry." Her voice came out hollow and echoey. It didn't sound like hers.

A female voice joined his, "Oh my gawd, what a scare. Thank God we found your purse. And your shoes." Christine looked over to see the lady from the concession stand watching her, worried. Her lipstick was a terrible color pink. Like bubblegum. She had too much on and her lips were pursed with concern. Christine thought how she could take this woman under her wing, show her the proper way to apply lipstick. Blackness again.

When Christine came to, the pain was less. She could tell by the smells before she opened her eyes that she was in a hospital. The pain in her limbs had subsided, but there was a new pain in her abdomen. Sharp cramping and a dull ache. She knew she was miscarrying, or she already had. She turned to her side to curl up but found that her wrists were held fast by something. She focused and saw that she was in restraints.

She saw Chuck sitting in the chair by the window. His face was furrowed, his hand pulling on his ear. When he saw that she was awake, his expression went from alarm to fear to sheer bafflement to anger.

He waggled his head back and forth. *When did his jowls get so loose?* His voice sounded hollow, hoarse in the small room. "What the hell, Christine? I mean what the *hell?*"

She didn't have anything to say to him. She wasn't supposed to be here. If she knew she'd known she going to be here, she might have had something to say.

monsters aren't under the bed: whiteness and sex (*an excerpt*)

by LIBRECHT BAKER

from *VETIVER*

example, picture of Sandra Bland in waller county, texas orange jumpsuit shrouding shoulders and chest against concrete backdrop, her sugar-glazed eyes un-alert and face slacken reflects photographer's camera's gaze—when are mugshots *not* taken in street clothes—mugshots show a person's revolting spirit, unless their stare is one of their spirit escaping a dying body

specimen ad nauseam, 2016 elections highlight our country's throbbing essence—divisiveness celebrated in the election of a trashbag president-elect, son of a white hood, how *pledge allegiance to the flag*, how sweet *bombs bursting in air*, how unripe lemon tangy, so spit into the hot multicultural pot holding our country's chunky organic-monsanto stew

sample, 40.2 percent of our poverty population is white-america, what is talk box saying, what is national newspaper informing about our poverty? only discussing poverty stricken people looking like deportation, a jail case, migratory, worth bordering, pepper spraying, to be slain, and what about the 40.2 percent—grief and hunger, an experienced shared in breath carried by wind

fear mongers greet 2016 election triumphant-deficit with a self-sworn badge to harass *the others* while waving ghost era flag that zombie forth eating statue of liberty's full, fleshy nose to a sliver—they've forgotten they're a handful of generations removed from immigrant status and their history is championed by the public educational system, but only some monsters read

is it to be afraid of *the others* and so needing *the others*—hungry for cultures, exoticism, seasoned foods with the tastes of certain histories—simultaneously the legacy of monsters and what happens when monsters doesn't comprehend their own monstrosity here, there's no question mark because onslaught has no end—this is part true of our america illustrated best where whiteness distracts us from ourselves or whiteness is too distracted from itself—its love, its history, its compassion—it/they/she/he have spent a long time trying to not remember and aide our memories' oblivion, but what would we expect from a *color* that is the end result of all colors spinning—has their spinning encouraged forgetting that roots grow in dark

selling brutality stories about us clashing with, assaulting, and murdering police, but what is more common is obvious—where police are present at peaceful rebellions so too is centuries of energy glimmering, off their dehydrated, piss color badge and riot gear—police bringing assault, murder, and clash against citizens, but what about the hungry 40.2 percent

and what about water, air, earth

america has always been great, no election or next president-elect can shift obvious fact that we are a country of immigrants—except the indigenous who know america's birth name(s)—however, generationally removed, the majority of us eat with a tongue split by its psychological diet where english has always been the forced first spoonful

monsters thrive by diverting incendiary focus. they are antebellum wannabes and as ugly as ever with a terror litany palette—america knows its terrorist candor and acts like the terrorists are the darkies over there, points finger, points finger and points finger across the sea, in the ghetto, shanty towns, places where survival seems to be thin and always fighting

Hechizo Para Congelar

by LI YUN ALVARADO

from *UNMARGIN*

for Mamá Merida who taught us the power of spells.

Ingredients:
1. Names
2. Pencil
3. Paper Bag
4. Freezer

Spell:
Pencil names onto
pieces of brown
paper bag.

Let's say:

donald john trump
kirstjen michele nielson
jefferson beauregard sessions III
sarah elizabeth huckabee sanders
immigrations and customs enforcement

Fold. Fold again.
Set intention. Speak:
que no hagan más

daño. Bury
tiny pieces in
freezer corner.

Wait for papers
to chill. Watch
as each person

freezes. Stopped
cold as

ICE, abolished.

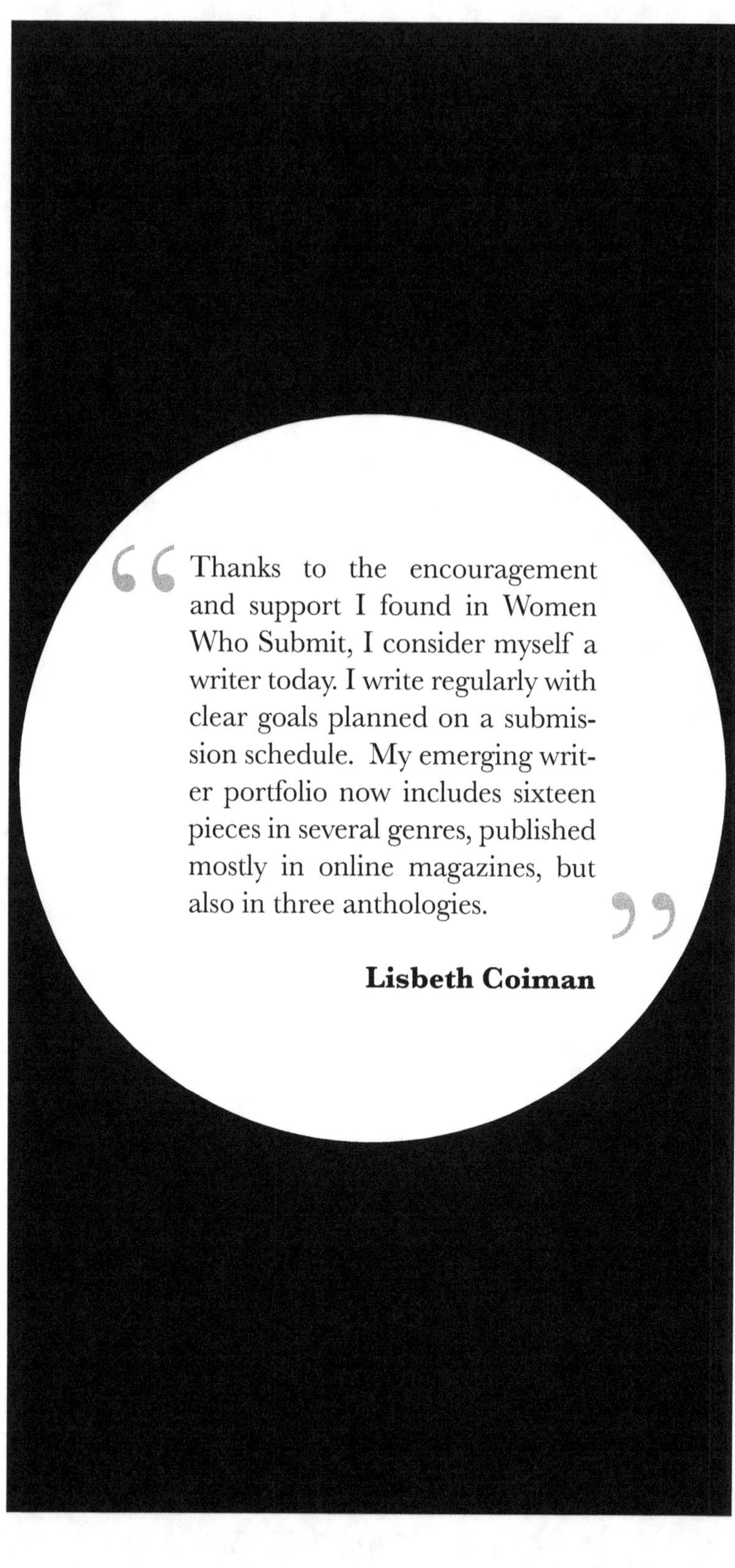
"Thanks to the encouragement and support I found in Women Who Submit, I consider myself a writer today. I write regularly with clear goals planned on a submission schedule. My emerging writer portfolio now includes sixteen pieces in several genres, published mostly in online magazines, but also in three anthologies."
Lisbeth Coiman

Nightmare on Elm Street

by CASSANDRA LANE

from *WRITERS RESIST*

Dylann Storm Roof invades my dream space in the days after he murders nine African Americans at a Bible study in Charleston, South Carolina.

His spirit travels 2,480 miles to reach the interior of my imagination in Los Angeles. Like a bloodhound, he finds my black Southern body hiding out in the desert. Terrorizing his victims and their families was not enough. Destroying the sanctity of a historically black house of worship was not enough. He comes for me, a girl who grew up kneeling beside her elders in anointed prayer at St. Paul Baptist Church on Elm Street.

Unshackled and smug, he comes for me. For us.

The dream begins under the cover of night, full of silence and a pregnant, starless sky. My heart pumps into this blackness. The blackness responds, alive and aware.

The scene switches to a clear afternoon, where sunlight slants between two buildings that stand on a hill. I am walking down a slope to pick my son up from school when I catch a glimpse of a man lurking next to a string of parked cars. He is wearing a soiled white t-shirt and jeans. Something in my spirit tells me that this man is wrong. All wrong.

I rush my son home, which turns out to be the home I grew up in on Elm Street in Louisiana. I am back in the South, after all. In the 1980s, this house was the object of constant teasing.

"It's Freddy Krueger's house," a couple of kids would yell day after day when the school bus pulled up to my house. "Yeah, and there's his girlfriend: Frederica!"

In my dream, I pause on the porch to finger the empty spot where the third address number should have been: 20_. Hear the ghost of the bus's screeching brakes and shrieking kids. I turn to look over my shoulder and see the gunman gaining on us. I yank open the front door that was always unlocked, get my son and myself inside and turn the deadbolt. Seconds later, Roof is at the door, rifle in hand.

As my son and I look for safe places to hide, I am both

terrified and furious. I want to ignore the possibility of death and unleash my rage on Roof's face, tear at his skin, a mask over hate.

He points his rifle. Its snout peers at the front door's window. He could easily shoot out the glass and work his way in. Instead, his strategy is to drag out the terror with painstaking patience and steadiness—tinkering with the door handle, making threats, stopping completely, and then starting up again. I hold the product of terror in my hands; it is in my son's small shoulders. His shoulders are bare and brown, full of naked fear.

I carry his tremors in my fingers, dialing first my husband and then the numbers that I have forgotten to constantly reiterate to my son: 9-1-1. In bursts of hysteria, I appeal to the operator: "He wants to kill us."

"Ma'am," the operator says—she is frighteningly calm—"someone is on the way to help you."

When the sheriff shows up, I look out the living room's side window, facing west. The sheriff and Roof stand outside the patrol car, face to face, their arms at their sides, relaxed.

Roof is now clad in a business suit—navy blue, immaculate. I see his rifle, hiding under the sheriff's car. I hear the sheriff talking to him in a low, calm tone. I make my way outside to get inside this, their intimate conversation.

With a screech, my husband drives up, jumps out of his car and lunges for the terrorist, but I lunge at him to restrain him. I envision the handcuffs glaring against his brown wrists. Click. Guilty. Assault. Attempted murder.

I hold him down and he holds me down, and in this holding, we begin, slowly, to regain our composure.

We are statues of self-restraint.

Elegy for the Orange

by ERIKA AYÓN

from *CULTURAL WEEKLY*

I peeled you on hot summer days,
let your skin fall on my lap.
Through you I shed my own skin,
shed myself for this new life in Los Angeles.
Your juice became my childhood nectar.
In California, you flourished in all seasons.
You were my light in the morning.
At night, you glimmered in the distance,
burned bright like a street lamp.
When I reached for you, I reached for the sun
that shined down on us as we stood around you,
waiting for the day to end, for the sun to set,
so my skin could cool, my eyes could rest.
I hold you as Apá offered triangles of you
spread out like a kaleidoscope on a plate.
When I blinked my eyes, you shifted shapes
in my head, my mind became dizzy.
You were my salvation. I exchanged you for
currency. Dollar bills handed to a little girl whose
hair curled at the ends, wore a pink headband,
and woke up in the middle of the night, wondered
where she was, forgot where she had come from.
Your fragrance followed me into schoolyards
where kids laughed at me for being seen with you
on the street corner. During lunch, I hid you
in the dark corners of my lunch bag.
I know I won't be your last survivor.
I see them every day at the entrance of the 110
Freeway, the man who holds you up
like a barbell. The woman who slices you into
small squares, mixes you into a fruit medley.
The couple that stands outside Jons Market,
presses you, pours you into clear cups,
turns your drops into dreams.

at the end of the devil's breath

by ROMAINE WASHINGTON

from *VOICEMAIL POEMS*

. . .july.
wilted cereal in a bowl / we
drown in brown boiling milk.
the haze of sparklers and fire-
works add to the deafening heat
that drips into

august.
caged in by smog,
air smells of cigarettes and melted tar.
surely this place is meant to
ignite.

september,
when he arrives,
he thinks this is a flat plain,
where desert dirt covers everything like snow
and sweat is meant for breathing.
but then-

october,
and the devil's breath laps up lotion,
claws skin with its vicious teeth.
yowling roofs beat whoosh and
bend of threatened windows.
tree leaves sound like ocean.
stripped-dry littered bare limbs.
the hard ones snap, ripe for a switch.
used-ta-be gangs of tumbleweeds ran the streets;
now, solitary wadded balls of rootless limbs roll by.

november
is a postcard miracle,
surrounded snow capped crisp sky

where our eyes hang glide like eagles.
we perch low in the valley shadow
straining to see
the walk of fame.
sunset and hollywood.
palm springs.
peer into the pier of the pacific.
every mountain peak is
paramount. he says,
if it weren't for the devil's breath,
i'd never know
where we are, and
just how beautiful.

Skid Row, 4 p.m.

by BONNIE KAPLAN

from *ICE CREAM POEMS*

There is screaming in the streets
below, sirens emanate
up seven floors to where I teach.
Every afternoon a crackling

tune draws closer, a relentless
loop of Pop Goes the Weasel.
The Ice Cream Man comes to Sixth
and San Pedro.

They still manufacture Bomb
Pops in striated flavors—cherry, lemon-
lime, and blueberry—summery,
sweet, dripping patriotism

all over the veteran's hand,
the one that still works.
Sometimes the Ice Cream Man
brings his son on the route.

The boy helps deliver Good
Humor Bars to those in wheelchairs,
and makes change. Grown-ups assemble
around the truck's window

for frozen Big Sticks,
Fifty-Fifty Bars, King Cones.
There is laughter and blue tongues
and a woman who thinks the Ice

Cream Man is stealing her thoughts—
the layers of peeling stickers
on his truck are evidence enough,
and how he keeps everyone coming back.

No aguanto: giving voice to our pain

by LETICIA URIETA

from *MIDNIGHT BREAKFAST*

There is a word in Spanish that comes back to me—aguantar. Strictly translated into English, it means to endure despite the weight of a negative force, but its usage can move across contexts. The one that I have heard most often—and from a woman's mouth—is the kind of pain, worry or sorrow that she is able to endure, and at what point her limits have been surpassed. As in, "no puedo aguantar mas." I cannot endure any more.

I learned this word from my paternal grandmother's mouth, in tears and in silence, as she endured, and then could no longer. Endured living with my verbally abusive father, as she had lived with my abusive grandfather before him. Endured the weight of how generational familial abuse weighed on the rest of the family. She let toxic machismo endure even as it was killing her.

Grandma's endurance was desperate silence, a cool demeanor. She was consistently abused, manipulated, and mistreated by people for much of her adult life. When her cheating husband was confronted by the husband of his lover as their family sat eating at a restaurant, Grandma calmly took the man aside, put her hand on his arm and asked him not to beat her husband in public in front of her children. Her hard-earned money cleaning houses for rich white families was often given away to her family who took advantage of her feelings of familial obligation. Until the stroke that unleashed an outspoken woman, my reserved Grandma applied her makeup and curled her hair every day, even when she could barely lift her hands above her head, even when it became difficult to live from month to month after my father took a good portion of her Social Security check.

In the nursing home, I listened to a scream so violent, it rattled Grandma's throat. It erupted whenever the nurses moved her from chair to bed, or had to change her clothes or give her a bath. She cursed them, and she cursed me and my cousins. She was louder at the end of her life than I had ever known her, leaping across English and Spanish to find the best words she knew for her pain, calling us malcriadas and bitches. On one particularly bad day, she insisted that someone was sawing off her leg, even though it sat perfectly still in her chair. From her bed, she pleaded with me in tears to make the nurses stop trying to move her. She seemed unconcerned that she had lifted her nightgown above her thigh to show me her still leg, insisting I look. "Mira mijita, mira lo que me estan hacienda," she told me, shaking her nightgown and willing me to see what was not there. Even when she calmed a few minutes later, her more placid tone was tempered by the accusation in her cloudy brown eyes.

I cried in the car on the way home. But I was glad, for once, to see this woman who had helped raise me finally be loud and unruly, when propriety had kept her quiet for so long.

*

In her book *The Body is Not An Apology: The Power of Radical Self-Love*, poet and author Sonya Renee Taylor asks the reader to engage in "radical reflections" about their relationship to their bodies and the bodies of others. When I began reading this book, I found myself responding to some of these prompts in the form of short journal entries. The one reflection that prompted the most writing from me was "In what ways have you been asked to apologize for your body?"

This was a question I had considered in other contexts, when I had been made to apologize for my weight, for how much room my body took up in a space, or for wearing clothing that was "too revealing" because of the way the curves of my body spilled out—even in clothing that would otherwise be considered modest. But this question of apology resonated with me more than ever as I was recovering from a sinus surgery. I'd had the surgery because I'd hoped it would alleviate two years of chronic migraines, nose bleeds and pain that had disrupted my life. As an adjunct professor with no contract, I had had to cancel classes—and risk future employment—because I could not leave my bed without becoming faint or vomiting. These moments wrenched control over my body and left me feeling helpless and childlike that I could do nothing to alleviate my suffering.

I am often told by doctors, specialists, dentists, and technicians that I am such a good patient because I don't flinch, scream, or flail when pierced by a needle, or when my nerves are drilled into and pain sensors flair and the blood comes after. The sad thing is I have always prided myself on being labelled a "good patient." I have done my best not to inconvenience the professionals who, I had always been taught, are the bastions of all medical truth.

During my sinus surgery, I woke up a few times under sedation. I have distinct bodily memories of the sharp, cold metal instruments working inside my nasal and sinus cavities, of the sound of my own moans for the surgeon to stop. Then darkness, and eventually waking and sobbing, as though the surgery had been a particularly intense dream I had slipped out of and back into the waking world. My rational brain could not comprehend why I was crying, and I silently scolded myself. It wasn't until I realized how much blood was pouring from my nose and the intense, face-shocking pain hit me, that I realized how much of the surgery I had felt, and how much more I was destined to feel. The anesthesiologist said, "I'm sorry that you woke up," but it sounded less like an apology and more like an accusation against my body's inability to surrender to the hands of doctors who, in the process of trying to fix me, had harmed me.

All too often, our pain is an inconvenience for those who have to treat us and care for our ailments.

Throughout this long treatment process, I thought of the stories my friends and family with chronic illnesses had told me. Of the ways in which they had been dismissed when their bodies did not respond to a linear treatment plan or expected outcome. A friend with Type 1 diabetes once recounted her seemingly endless saga to lose weight and lower her A1C levels, despite altering her diet and exercise habits. Her doctor consistently shamed her for the lack of change in her levels, repeatedly asking, "What are we going to do about this?" In a last-ditch effort to affect these levels, her doctor prescribed her a medication that would supposedly help, though its primary side effects are nausea and diarrhea. As my fatigued friend told the story, she threw her hands up, frustrated that her trusted endocrinologist had prescribed a glorified laxative because her condition was more her fault than his.

As I navigated the saga of my own pain, I found myself drawn to the stories of other women whose pain had been dismissed by the medical community, and whose voices were declaring this pain as part of themselves, despite the attempts to silence them.

In her latest collection of poetry and essays, *Night-Blooming Jasmin(n)e*, Jasminne Méndez chronicles her experiences and struggles as an Afro-Latina woman with pericardial effusion and pericarditis that has affected her throughout her adult life. In one essay, she responds to a nurse who attempts to dismiss her concerns:

> I lifted my shirt and pants and was hooked up to an EKG

machine because I was once again in the ER complaining of chest pains and shortness of breath. The nurses asked for my health insurance card, and there began the usual flurry of activity I had come to expect in these cases of emergency.

Velcro ripped on the blood pressure machine, vitals checked, machines beeped, the paper curtain rustled open and closed behind me. I stood on the scale, answered inane questions and explained why the pulse ox-meter said I was not breathing.

"I have Raynaud's. You're not going to get an accurate reading from my fingers." The young white female nurse in baby blue scrubs looked at me and said, "You're too pretty to be this sick."

I stared at the retro tiled floor annoyed by her comment. "Thank you, but clearly lupus doesn't care how pretty I am."

Méndez's words are more than an account of pain made invisible by youth, beauty, and perceived "normalcy." They are a declaration in the face of this pain when no one wants to hear it. Considering the way that women of the African diaspora have historically had their pain dismissed by the medical community, this honest witnessing of her own pain is necessary. This passage reminds me of times when my youth or perceived health caused doctors or nurses to dismiss the severity of my pain. For a period in my late twenties, I was told that an irregular swooping feeling in my chest, close to my heart, were just symptoms of anxiety that doctors see in "women your age," even when I iterated that this felt different than a panic attack. After several EKGs and chest scans, I still don't know why this happens to me. I struggled to insist on my pain or discomfort, or on my needs as Méndez had, but I am reminded of how necessary it is to speak our truths even when these gatekeepers of health don't want to hear it.

*

In her book, Taylor explains how living in our bodies often disrupts the default understanding of what a body should be, including the assumption that it should be healthy and free from pain. Before my surgery, health had always been something I thought of as an achievement, something to strive for because without this effort, what was the alternative? As I heard the voices of the women who have been struggling longer than me, and who had to be their own advocates in a system that wanted their silent conformity, it became clear just how much I had relinquished control over how my body had been treated in the past.

At twenty-four, I experienced my first UTI. I was a kindergarten teacher entering my third year of teaching, and on the day before school would start, I was busy at work readying my materials and classroom for my incoming students. Because I had never had an infection like it before, I waited until the pain was so bad that I rushed from my unfinished classroom to the bathroom at least four times and urinated blood. Later, at the hospital with my husband, I quietly snuck off to the restroom every three minutes. Urinating felt like passing particles of glass through my urethra, and each time I went I felt that something irreversible was happening to me.

My husband and I waited four hours before I was finally able to see a nurse. Despite the excruciating discomfort written on my face, the extent of my infection was not taken seriously until I handed the nurse a sample of my urine that was black with blood. Taking it from my hand, she muttered, "Oh my god," and I was rushed into a room to receive antibiotics. Later, an ER doctor told me that the infection had caused my bladder to hemorrhage, and that it was close to infecting my kidneys. After this experience I went to the restroom more regularly and took cranberry pills, but more than anything I took with me the sense that remaining "brave" in the face of my own pain might kill me.

I understand that it is difficult for medical professionals to truly understand their patient's pain when they are not experiencing the pain themselves. It is a struggle that continues without radical acts of empathy from medical professionals and other caretakers. This problem continues when doctors and specialists treat ailments as individual issues, rather than looking at a patient's health holistically. What happens when pain or illness is not evident? To what extent must illness be proven?

I was recently told by a particularly good massage therapist that she felt a lump in my left thigh. She had been working the muscles in my legs for fifteen minutes before she informed me in a calm voice, so as not to startle me and ruin the rest of the session. When I went to my general practitioner, he spent less than five minutes feeling the lump through my jeans before pronouncing it "most likely benign." My mortal fear was such an inconvenience to his busy schedule, that he could not even be bothered to examine the lump further before stating his approximate diagnosis. He recommended that I get an ultrasound of the lump, just to be sure.

During the procedure, I lay bare-bottomed on the chair

while the tech poured gel on my thigh and complained that the lump was difficult to discern from the muscle surrounding it. The tech then left me in this vulnerable state, noting that the doctor, whom I had never met, could enter the room with me like this at any time to consult the image. I was then told to just sit tight. And I did so, without complaint. Though the lump was confirmed to be benign, the experience was yet another reminder that my well-being and comfort were secondary to the procedures of the radiologists who cared for me.

There are too many stories of women insisting on their needs for treatment, only to be dismissed and sent home. Some of them die because they are misdiagnosed or wrongfully labelled "anxious" and "hysterical." Some of them return and insist on saving their own lives. Many of these dismissals are rooted in a long history of patriarchal attempts to control women's bodies and therefore our understanding of our own bodies. We are not often taught to be our own advocates until we are given no other choice. It bleeds into the ways we endure across all areas of our lives—how we are willing to endure toxic work places, abusive relationships, and unhappiness in many forms, but are quick to tell other women that they don't deserve this kind of suffering.

I have only now begun to contend with the ways I have failed to be my own advocate. Despite advocating for the voices of others, I have abdicated my responsibility to care for myself to the expertise of those who would treat and label my body as they saw fit. Each time I suppressed my bodily instincts to shout, rebel or run, my body learned that it was separate from my consciousness, and no longer free. How could I have compassion for others, but none for myself?

*

I continue to be inspired by women who refuse to suppress their pain for the sake of others' comfort. During the act of writing this essay, I questioned whether I even had a right to recount my own struggles. Did my pain qualify? The more I read and the more I listened, I began to understand that I was situating myself in a conversation that I hope will not soon end.

When writer and cultural critic Roxane Gay curated and contributed to a series of essays called *Unruly Bodies* at Medium, I read these pieces every week, feeling particularly seen with each one. One such essay by Carmen Maria Machado, "Unruly, Adjective," speaks to her daily existence in her body, listing her pains, her ailments, and the many parts of her that make up a body which will not fall in line. Her essay ends with this glorious statement:

> "I do not hate my body, because such a thing would be pointless, shortsighted. You cannot hate an animal for what she is, especially one who bears your ungrateful mind through this terrible world. And anyway, how do you hate something who marks her territory so dramatically, with such violence and panache? Who reminds you, with each step, I am here, I am here, I am here?"

The way that Machado illustrates the power of her body in its free expression of imperfection and pain is beautiful, and haunting. While reading, I thought of a question in the last chapter of Taylor's book that I am still asking myself: "If you decide to be at war with your body, how will you ever have peace?"

After my sinus surgery, I had to get three fillings at the insistence of my dentist. Throughout the procedure, the dentist and dental hygienist seemed to be in a tug-of-war with my mouth until my cheeks stretched so far out, I wondered if they would ever return to their original shape. I clenched my fists and sighed to express the intensity of the pain inflicted by the inch-long needle sinking into my gums. The hygienist patted my arm and told me to breathe through my nose, which, because of the previous surgery, was congested beyond breath. In her Northern Mexican accent, she told me "it's okay Mamá" every time I struggled, coughed, or flinched, and each time she did I felt less comforted and more betrayed. She was asking me to stifle my pain because to gurgle and flinch made her have to look away.

I wonder what Grandma would say to this woman who attempted to calm me in the language of my familia, as if she were my ally. I imagine her raising her weak hand with yellowing, claw-like nails and slapping the woman across the face.

No, no más. I will not endure.

Heaven Make Me a Warrior to Slay All the Bad Magic

by LAUREN EGGERT-CROWE

from *BLACK WARRIOR REVIEW*

your voice in me
and then the ghost
of your voice
in me

Spent my last nickels
on your pretty blues

Vexing declaratives, honey-tongued
& fortune: I am still, I am

still, I am still
furious as a boxed up

zephyr. Make me make
you regret coming

towards me and my barred
elbows. Sideways thunder
on a Thursday.

Interview Questions

by DANIELLE MITCHELL

from *ANIMAL*

Question: Will you let this bird sit on your lap?

Define boundary.

Define the smell of a dead
volcano.

Question: What is a gathering of victims,
murder or herd?

Question: Could we call this a convict of roses?

Define the difference between quiz
& testament.

True or False: The dream gave you instructions.

Female suffering: An answer or a question?

Question: Why do you refuse to obey
your instructions?

Define being endangered.

Scotland: The green is so green
it is actually onions.

If you wake from this it will all
have been a test. True or False.

The Lady of the Watch

by HAZEL KIGHT WITHAM

from *NONBINARY REVIEW*

It was an exquisite moment the night I realized I was the Lady of Shalott. She was the heroine of a favorite poem by Alfred Lord Tennyson, a poem that first came to me from a red-haired actress playing one of my literary heroines. The Lady was a woman imprisoned in a tower above Camelot. She sat at her loom night and day, and could only look at a reflection of the world through a mirror because

> *she has heard a whisper say,*
> *a curse is on her if she stay,*
> *to look down to Camelot.*

So the lady sits and weaves, unable to even glance down at the world, until one day bold Sir Lancelot flashes into the mirror and she forgets herself, forgets the curse, and dares to look out to Camelot.

By the end of the poem the Lady of Shalott, "half-sick of shadows," has found a boat and sets out into the real world, only to have her blood frozen wholly before Sir Lancelot happens upon her, notices how pretty she is, and how dead.

The night the Lady possessed me I didn't have access to books of poetry, so I recited it from memory as I stripped off my scrubs and stripped down the bed. Some part of me had wanted to be her since childhood when I first read, then watched, as the fiercely adventurous Anne of Green Gables reenacted Tennyson's poem with her friends. Anne laid herself down in a boat, clutched flowers, accepted farewell kisses from her mates, then shoved off to drift poetically along the river until her blood was "frozen wholly." I disregarded the moment in the scene when Anne's boat is swamped and she frantically tries to bail herself out before abandoning ship and jumping onto a bridge piling, soaked and sorry as a drenched cat. And then she has to accept rescue from none other than that damn Gilbert Blythe, who just happens upon her in a borrowed dory.

I didn't want to acknowledge my own cursed tower, my own sinking ship, my desperate need for rescue. I didn't want to continuously dwell in the fact that I should be starting my sophomore year of college, instead of being confined here, in this place of cinderblocks and metal beds. I just wanted to live inside the bars of that poem the way Anne did, instead of the bars of the cage I kept waking up in, day after day.

Willows whiten, aspens quiver,
Little breezes, dusk and shiver
Through the wave that runs for ever
By the island in the river
Flowing down to Camelot.

Four gray walls, and four gray towers,
Overlook a space of flowers,
And the silent isle imbowers
The Lady of Shalott.

Inside my four white walls I wound the flat sheet around me to create a long, flowing white gown with just a hint of the turquoise Kaiser Permanente lettering down one side. I tore off the fitted sheet and twirled it around my head so it created looping, curling tresses my mind painted red. Last was the standard issue knit blanket, cream and stripped of all softness, offering little warmth. I draped it around my shoulders and kicked off my booties, which were to be worn at all times. Then:

She left the web,
She left the loom,
She made three paces thro' the room…

and I stepped out into the purple-blue carpeted riverbed of the hallway.

My fellow captives were assembled in the lounge, each wearing the exact same blue scrubs I had recently removed, distracted by a screening of *Ace Ventura: Pet Detective.* I draped myself across the corner of the couch and the townsfolk's faces came alive. While Courtney Cox made dolphin noises, I snapped them from their complacency and they too looked like they wanted to rise up and shed the garments of their captivity.

It was only minutes before the night nurses descended. They told me I couldn't walk around without any clothes on, and I was outraged. I wasn't naked, I was the Lady, I was beautiful, and who was I hurting?

But the powers that be did not see it that way. They escorted me back to my room and made me change back into those dreaded scrubs and the damn booties. They gave me a pill to rein in the side of me that liked to act out.

Later that night I snuck out of my room and tried to break free of my tower. I flew down the purple-blue river and slammed into the big window at the end of the hall. I held counsel with the glass, trying to convince it to set me free, let me go, release me to spill out into the lamplit night and the dewdamp grass. It didn't budge. Night Nurse marched after me and hauled me back to my room. I did that trick learned from countless Nancy Drews where you go limp, act like you're beaten and compliant, but when nurse's grip relaxed I tore back down the hall cackling and howling. Then it was four or five staff members who carried me back, bucking and brawling, strapped me down on the bed, and injected me with something that smacked me into true compliance.

*

When I returned to college that spring it was on pills that disguised me as someone more Anne than Lady, someone normal and sane, someone who hadn't spent close to eight weeks under lock and key, convinced I'd never again see the outside. I had been terrified I had lost my life, that I was doomed to waste away inside a place where there was decidedly no scope for the imagination. So it was with a rush of gratitude and anticipation that I returned to the school of my dreams, that wild open sky so far from home. But rather than the wide-eyed and overeager Anne I had been in the first weeks of my freshman adventure, I was the abashed Anne, the sorry, cold, drenched and dripping Anne, the Anne who was chilled by a secret shame. When I petitioned the dean of Res Life to return I was the mannered Anne, the sobered and responsible Anne. I was not going to be borrowing boats or becoming Ladies.

I played responsible so well I got the okay to resume studies, despite the school's standard policy that medical leaves due to psychiatric issues require a full year off. Elated, I began setting up my new dorm room, unpacking all the boxes friends had packed up while I was busy going crazy in the fall. From one I pulled out a rolled-up poster of a painting by Waterhouse and spread it open on the bed. In it a forlorn woman is drifting in a boat, her long red hair loose, her white clothes flowing around her. She has a tapestry across her lap. Around the prow is written: *The Lady of Shalott.*

It was like falling into a mirror. I looked at her across the expanse that separates fact and fiction, prose and poetry, sanity and madness, astonished she would find me again. This woman who had liberated herself from her prison, only to have the curse of leaving fall upon her. She sought freedom with nothing holding her but a borrowed boat and some warmth she'd woven thread by thread in that loom-laden cage. Her face is stricken, her body rigid with fear of what is to come. She frees herself only to freeze herself under a wild open sky.

Tennyson never writes why the Lady is cursed, or why she had to be locked away to begin with. My own curse was equally unclear, and who I was upon release was a mystery. But something in the Lady's story compelled Anne to experiment with reckless escapes, and something in the poem and Anne's reenactment of it freed me for a brief time in the hospital, and then saw me out again, soaked and sorry, drenched with shame. And now, the question: what would happen to my own hard fought freedom? Would it crush me, curse me, freeze me too?

I taped the Lady up on my dorm's cinderblock wall, where she would keep watch over me that whole stumbling spring semester. Frozen there on my wall, her face stretched in terrible knowing as she drifts toward death. She was my shadow self, the one that echoed reminders as I tried to leave behind the shame and secret of my tower, that cage meant to keep me safe. I held on to the knowledge that I could slip, if I wasn't lucky enough to be rescued, into deeper, colder waters I might not emerge from.

She stayed with me, stilled in that sad moment of release and regret, and kept watch those long lonely months as I slowly navigated my way back into the world I knew I could so easily drift away from.

Waiting

by TANYA KO HONG

from *PALOS VERDES LIBRARY DISTRICT ANTHOLOGY*

When I think of you, rain comes
When I call you, you come in rain
When I touch you, you disappear
in rain

Bring me raw garlic and a handful
of bitter green wormwood
I will eat them and stay in a cave
21 days, 100 days
that's how bear became woman
I will do the same
If I can see you one last time.

There is another myth—
When you fold one thousand paper cranes,
your dream comes true.
If I can see you one last time
I will fold thousands—
ten thousand paper cranes.

I want to open your apartment door again
with the key that you sent by mail,
the key still warm from your hand,
hang my clothes in your closet between your clothes—
I want to feel safe there again.

Waiting for you is nothing—
Without blinking, I watch
the night become silver rain in blue light

I will wait for you like a rock on the water line
wishing you to be a wave and reach me—
If you touch,
I will collapse and be water like you.

Neptune Neptune Omega

by LISA RICHTER

from *MONTHS TO YEARS*

I'm sitting in our garden wrapped in a quilt, my body warmly protected, my head exposed to smacking gusts of chilled air. The weather has turned; a storm is blowing in. Adrienne Rich's collection of prose, *On Lies, Secrets, and Silence* rests by my side. I've returned to this book several times over the past years; its pages are marked with comments, story starts, my own spontaneous poems. I open the book to find an oh! in the margin beside a passage I've underlined. *The liar*, it begins, *leads an existence of unutterable loneliness.*

I consider what part of my life might be a lie, perhaps to some degree most, for my body has lied to my mind, my mind to my body, and I think of Lyn during her years of treatment, how we never talked about the end, for it wasn't going to happen, how her doc never mentioned the end for it wasn't going to happen, and how my mind told my body that it wasn't going to happen, though my body knew the truth, and hadn't Lyn, too?

Lying is done with words, Adrienne writes, *and also with silence.*

Tucked between pages of the book, I find a loose-leaf sheet folded into a neat rectangle. It is wide-ruled, three-holed. Pale blue horizontal lines, one long thin vertical red. I unfold the paper, and with it the memory. Three simple words stacked one atop each other, a list written with care in loopy cursive, the *p* connected to the *t*, the *t* to the *u*.

1 Neptune
2 Neptune
3 Omega

The shock of these words. The uselessness of uncovering them now, six months later. I don't recall stashing them here; how strange to have silenced them within these pages urging the spoken truth.

*

Her name was Marie. She'd had hair dyed the color of butter and shaped in a teased style—rolled bangs, puffed out sides smoothed stiff with spray—a look which dated her and made her somewhat unreal. She was the second try of hospice at our home; the first, Carol, had arrived with a pitying look and an "I'm sorry I'm here..." and was sent packing immediately.

The discussed plan was to use hospice *just for a while*, until Lyn recovered from the lung surgery, to eliminate for a couple days (maybe weeks) the exhausting drives back and forth to the hospital. It had been my suggestion, impelled by awaking to Lyn's gasps for air in the middle of the night, panics which terrorized us both. Just for a while, I'd promised Lyn, though our parents had been in hospice and our experience spoke otherwise. *Just for a while*, though for them, as for nearly all, it had been a one-way passage. Marie offered encouragement. "We have had patients who've entered our care," she emphasized to Lyn, "then left, then sometimes came back in, then left again. It requires a little bit of paperwork, that's all." A sympathetic shrug, a tight smile.

Alone with Marie afterwards, outside where I am now, I remember pointing out a cluster of magnolia blossoms birthed just that morning, their velvety white petals falling open like bowls, cupping the sun's glowing warmth. Marie didn't look. She took a blank sheet of paper from a folder and uncapped a black pen and this is what she said:

When it is over, here is who you call.

Her tone was abrupt, but not harsh. She was, I reasoned, being professional. Death was her specialty.

"Neptune," Marie said as she wrote the name of the mortuary following the numeral "1" on the lined paper, a sizable diamond and a diamond-inlaid wedding band flashing on her hand. "It was a family business once. Terrible sibling feud. They split, yet each kept the name." On the line below she wrote a numeral "2" followed by "Neptune" again. "Either will do..." she said. She paused and then went ahead with the story. "Some of our patient families aren't aware that there are two...and both local. It's happened that they've called one for the pickup and accidentally been connected to the other for the ashes and been informed the body isn't there, was never there." She chuckled as she wrote Omega down as a third option. This was not funny. I wanted to tell her she needed to leave, but then Lyn called from inside and Marie got up to tend to her.

After a couple minutes, I followed Marie downstairs to our bedroom.

There had been many firsts, but metering out morphine in

a syringe to my love came along unexpected. *Roxynol*, it was called. Marie drew a picture of a sucker and a bottle, using the same careful movements with which she'd written the names of the mortuaries. "Give her, when she needs it, .25," she said to me, explaining its position on the gauge. "That is ¼ the way up. The center is .5." She studied my face, touched my hand. Her job involved interacting daily with people like me, the numbed ones who loved, who stood by and watched and waited, who eventually nodded yes to the worst of news.

When Lyn died one week later, our friend Andy picked up the phone and called the local mortuary, McCormick and Sons, a fake stone façade building on a gravel lot with a small fountain in the front. It was to this sullen place we went the following day, he by my side, to sit in the office and discuss the options: the cost of Lyn's cremation, when it would take place, which vessel would contain her ashen remains.

Who are you? The woman hovering in the mortuary's vapid front room wanted to know. During the preceding years of hospital visits and chemo treatments, everyone had wanted to know. *You a relative? A friend?* "Her partner," I'd say, and they'd nod—whether doctor, nurse, or undertaker—and they'd know that legally this meant nothing, but heart-wise it meant I was being ripped in half.

I filled out the cremation forms, signed them, spoke a couple yes's and no's, maybe a thank you at the end, Andy there, gentle witness, holding steady for me. I wrote a check, and we left, terrorized. "You did good," he said.

Would Neptune, Neptune, or Omega have been any different? Any less harrowing than the goth woman who opened the door of the mortuary when I returned to pick up Lyn's ashes? Black gypsy cloth, dyed raven hair, a face as bland and colorless as moon dust, the foyer in which she stood, an unlit gray. She slid the canister across a wooden desk toward me, pushing it with the tips of her fingers. The voice rasping in her throat said "Sign, and you can go."

"I'm sorry," Lyn had said just a week earlier to friends when they came to visit before departing on a trip; they'd brought birthday cards and candles for her 60th birthday which was, in fact, *this* day, the day I cradled the small canister of her ashes in my arms.

"I'm sorry, baby," was all I could think to say as I settled the canister in the car's trunk, propped between books and boxes for the ride home. *I'm sorry*. Not an apology but an admission of utter helplessness. The ultimate surrender of nothing more to give.

*

A puff of wind descends in an exhausted sigh. I refold the loose-leaf sheet and return it to Adrienne's book, its pages flipping softly beside me.

We never said goodbye.

How does one utter the inconceivable? Our farewells during the final weeks took the form of spontaneous guttural wails, begun by Lyn and joined in by me, indulged for a couple moments then halted as swiftly as they'd taken hold.

I've saved some of Lyn's phone messages, listening to them when I feel strong enough, when the crave of their comfort is greater than the sadness I know they will also bring. Her faith was unshakable. In one of the last recordings, she confides in her characteristic sanguine tone that she's just awoken and is breathing somewhat freer, the aches are somewhat less, perhaps things have finally turned around. She pauses, an intimacy. Then the whisper, *I love you*, her words absolute.

What Scattered in the Wind

by REBECCA GOMEZ FARRELL

from *LITTLE LETTERS ON THE SKIN*

Hollow rasps of laughter pestered her to wakefulness. Any noise would have done the same, though she clamped her eyelids together in protest. For years, Ruth had heard nothing but the teakettle's hiss or the slow scrape of her cane against the camper's floor panels. The creaking sound of her voice rarely interrupted the silence. Unlike the other wayfarers, Ruth had never developed the habit of talking to herself. She didn't care to hear what she'd have to say.

"*Hee-hee, hee-he-heee!*"

Ruth plugged her ears, but it did no good, the laughter too sharp, too loud. Too out of place in this canyon between unnamed mesas. She drew the powder-blue afghan around her shoulders, a shell pattern she'd crocheted the last winter. In a few more months, she'd burn it on the grill, watch through narrowed eyes as embers chased each thread. It was a way to mark seasons in a place without trees, to remind herself that the world cycled on and she took up space within it.

"*Hee-he-hee, hee!*"

Her eyes fluttered open. She toyed with pretending at sleep for a moment longer, but that wouldn't do—Ruth had never shirked from what life threw in her path. Except that once, so long ago she could not say when it might have been.

Slats of light sheared through the blinds. She shrugged the blanket off, rose in an ivory-colored slip. A yellowed knit shawl remained on a hook by the stove, one of its unraveled threads hanging low enough to catch flame. Breath caught in her ribcage at the sight of it. Once, a man in blue, a shield pinned on his chest, had asked her questions of it, and she'd feigned absentmindedness, that she knew. Now, she could not recall the circumstances.

She opened the door.

The RV groaned as her weight shifted off the last metal step, sun-blindness taking a minute to blink away. Another trailer had pulled in down by the trickle of a stream. A fresh coat of red dust rose two feet up its exterior. Raised letters spelled *Chieftain* on its side, the same model as Ruth's rusty old camper. Beyond it, a child ran in wild circles, stopping for tickles from a mother whose lawn chair sat close to the sun-cracked ground.

Scratchy with disuse, Ruth's voice sounded as painful to her ears as the boy's laughter. "Where'd you come from?"

The boy's bouncy black curls fell still as his head followed her vibration. Where eye sockets once had been, vacant crevices sizzled with licks of flame.

Ruth swallowed her gasp of recognition with a scowl. It had been so many years since she'd seen him. Enough years to baste and rend the veil of age again, to twist lies into the truths she'd told herself.

The mother rose. A bright white shawl fell from her shoulders, crumbling to ashes in the wind. The boy reached for her hand, and the two visitors melded together, flesh fusing to sticky flesh. Ruth recognized the mirth lines she'd once worn on the mother's face, the freckles on her nose. They marked skin that dissolved as mother and child advanced, sparking dust devils of detritus that danced to the desert floor. A different question came to Ruth's lips, the one she'd had no answer for when all this had begun. "Why'd you come?"

"We've always been here," said the mother. "You've just forgotten."

Ruth spat at the ground. "No, no. I just wish you'd never been."

Enflamed tissue uncoupled from the child's arm like black grains from white in a flipped sandscape. Smoke brought tears to Ruth's eyes, but she held her ground, even as the child's searing grasp brought the familiar sickly stench of her torment.

Ruth had never shirked from what life threw in her path. Except that once.

Except that once.

Peanut Poem

by FLINT

from *A QUIET COURAGE*

There's nothing else you can do
when eating a peanut.   Nothing
but the crack & the clever cleft
a salty seedpod of delight.
No book in hands too busy to hold
the
    wandering
            words.

Just you
    & the tiny world
delivering salty babies & you
         Zeus
happily eating the children.

Abundance Guilt

by LISBETH COIMAN

from *NAILED MAGAZINE*

Along the wide corridors of the wholesale store, I look for the basic ingredient of my favorite dish, Pabellón Criollo. Flank steak is a piece of lean meat that once cooked can be shredded like strands of yarn. The refrigerators burst with a large variety of large meat cuts. My shopping cart bumps into others. The shoppers mutter apologies; try samples of hot tamales, Italian sausage, and Indian curry. Hips of fresh fruits and vegetables seem to smile from across the vast space. It's almost repugnant to see so much food.

Twice a week, in Venezuela, my 80-year-old father lines up to buy his ration of food: chicken and split rice. When he arrives, the line is already a couple of miles long. But with his cane, his white hair, and his insecure steps, he has earned the privilege to go to the front of the crowd. He hasn't earned the right of safety, though. When hours later, the angry mob decides to break in and take the food, they stampede over my father. Somebody rescues him, but not his glasses. He escapes with just a few bruises.

I set up two large pressure pots on my stove, one for the meat and one for the black beans. In the meat pot, I throw in a whole onion, garlic, a red bell pepper, a few whole peppercorn, whole allspice, and three cloves. In the bean pot go two pounds of black beans, an onion cut in quarters, and a whole green bell pepper. I close the lids, and wait for the whistles to announce that I should reduce the heat, and put up with the noise for the next half hour, the only inconvenience in the preparation of food in my house in the USA. I sit down with my coffee and text my sister back home. "I'm not feeling well," I said, embarrassed to announce that I'm cooking Pabellón.

My brother sends my mother food via cargo from Miami, which yields as long as she can stretch it, but that's not enough. I have sent money on occasions, but it doesn't make much difference either because the problem is not only lack of money. Simply put, there is no food to buy. Fortunately, there are mangoes, but even the mango trees are suffering from over harvesting. There is nothing else to eat. There are already reports of people losing weight for lack of food.

While the pots whistle, I prepare the sofrito for the beans. In Venezuela, I would have blended onion, green bell pepper, garlic, and parsley. But I feel like chopping is better today. I want to take time, reflect a bit on how fortunate I am, meditate almost on the fact that despite my difficulties as an immigrant in the USA, I am fortunate, safe, well fed. In a frying pan, I cook chopped ham. Once it's golden, I remove it from the pan, and add corn oil, and the vegetables. Once the onion is translucent, I add salt and pepper, a dash of cumin, and place the mixture in the bean pot, along with the ham. I let it simmer for another 20 minutes at medium heat. I rub my neck, tired from bending over the kitchen counter.

It wasn't always that way in Venezuela, a country of abundance: luscious landscape, year round supply of exotic fruits and vegetables, fertile soil, rich in minerals that make the country one of the largest reservoirs of oil in the world. Yet, Venezuela is hungry today.

Hugo Chavez won the election by a landslide, with 80% of the popular vote, in 1999, two years after I left Venezuela. I never liked the man because I have a natural distrust for the military, even more so, for an army man who attempted two coup d'etats to a sitting president (not that I particularly liked that president either), and who had an incendiary discourse to begin with. After the first attempted coup, the media flocked to Chavez' cell and made him a celebrity, for his supposed courage. From the jail, he became a charismatic and demagogic political figure. He promised to put the corrupt politicians before the firing squad in the Olympic stadium. The crowds roared. I was happy I had taken my children out of the country by then.

While the beans become a soup, I deal with the meat: let it cool, and then painstakingly separate each strand by pulling with the tip of my fingers. In a large pot, I throw in onion and garlic. After the onion has "cried," I add chopped red bell pepper and sweet banana peppers. A minute later, in go the chopped tomatoes, two spoonful of ketchup, and Worcestershire sauce. I let this vegetable mixture boil and then simmer for 20 minutes, after which I season with salt, pepper, cumin, and cayenne pepper. Then I add the shredded meat, and a cup of the stock.

In 2002, after serious confrontation for his oil program for Cuba, Chavez went against the oil company that has fed the country well for generations. Petróleos de Venezuela, PDVSA, had been the country's first employer and main checking account since it was nationalized in the 70s. Chavez dismantled the entire company, and 50,000 oil workers went abroad and today serve powerful oil companies in the US, Belgium, UK, France, Russia, and China. Those who remain drive taxi cabs on the streets of Venezuela's major cities. By that time, the government turned regime established a fierce price control policy, creating a great deal of friction with the manufacturing industry, food producers, and retailers.

It's hot and humid in my kitchen, where it smells like my tropical childhood: freshly squeezed orange juice, bread pudding in the oven, coffee brewing, and parchita (passion fruit). I call my husband to ask him to bring plantain from the ethnic store near the refinery where he works. I check both the meat and the beans for seasoning.

In 2005, Chavez implemented the expropriation of unproductive farms, with the idea of redistributing to increase food production and fight rural poverty. In reality, the expropriation law became a political weapon to confiscate land from his opponents and gain absolute control of the heartland. The seized property was fenced with giant posters that showed a romantic idea of the future productive land. Years later, a reporter trespassed those fences with a video camera to show the world the idle land overgrown with weeds. The expropriated landowners left the country, if they could, or went into the resistance, if they couldn't.

When the beans are ready, I remove them from the stove, where I place a smaller pot with water for the rice. I add salt and corn oil and let the water boil. Then I add two cups of par boiled rice, see it boil, then immediately reduce the heat and cover. Something pulls from inside my stomach, it feels like hunger, and I tell myself I have to wait until the meal is ready. I check the news in my phone, news about another demagogue, one with funny hair. I cringe.

What was born out of the Cuban model of land redistributions was used against political opponents to confiscate their property, houses, or factories, even merchandise from retailers. Industries that wanted to stay on top of their game played low and seemed complacent with the regime. It took longer to get to Empresas Polar. This food producing company started as a brewery in Caracas in 1941 and became the country's second employer behind PDVSA. The conglomerate produces beer, malt, soft drinks, juices, corn flour (our staple), rice, pastas, margarines, corn oil, cheese spreads, jellies, tuna fish, and frozen sea food.

With the rice ready, I turn off the stove, wash all the utensils, wipe the kitchen, and sweep the floor. Then turn off the kitchen lights and go to my upstairs office to write. I love the comfort and safety I enjoy, the luxury of having space to live and work.

Withholding payment from creditors became another political strategy, and since the country produces oil but not enough food for its people, it also must import all raw materials and pay in dollars, a currency heavily controlled by the state. Without payment, the food supply started to dwindle. The more regulated the product, the more scarce it was: milk, meat, chicken, and toilet paper, sanitary napkins, diapers, condoms, and medicine in general. Meanwhile, Empresas Polar has been quietly feeding the country, if only with bare essentials. But in 2016, the growing tension between the dictator and the food company reached the breaking point. Unable to pay for imported raw material in the currency-controlled country, Polar confronted the government, which in turned accused the food producer of conspiring with the empire (USA) and called in the military to confiscate the factories. No more food.

When he died, Chavez named a successor, as if he were a king. At least Chavez was intelligent. Nicolas Maduro is inept beyond reason, and with ineptitude and ignorance comes cruelty. He laughs on live TV at the images presented to him by journalists of people scavenging garbage bins for leftover food. There is no productivity left in a country that has to line up for hours a day, several days a week, for a ration of food. There is no dignity left either.

While I sip a shot of Venezuelan rum, I remember last Christmas when a group of Venezuelans invited my husband and me to dinner. We shared the table with oil engineers from our country, their wives, and children, and ate the delicate dishes that make our Christmas: Hallacas, pan de jamón, pernil, and ensalada de gallina, the abundance with which we all grew up. I think I caught the flu that night because I haven't been feeling well since.

Venezuela's largest bill is the 100 Bolivares, today worth 0.02 cents of a dollar. Once deemed useless, the bill should have been replaced immediately. Five days before Christmas, Nicolas Maduro ordered the recall of the bill, but didn't replace it. People burnt the useless money on the streets. No food and no money. In the course of 18 years, the country went from the first economy of the subcontinent, to a level of poverty known only to Haiti.

I dress up the table, serve the Pabellón Criollo: carne mechada, black beans, white rice, and fried plantain. I set up fork and knife, and a simple white napkin. In front of me, a glass of clear, clean water, and a shot of rum, Santa Teresa, Anniversary version.

But I can't eat. Guilt of abundance shuts down my stomach, and I weep.

Invasive Species

by JENNIFER BARONE

from *FORUM, LITERARY MAGAZINE OF CCSF*

we forge a space for ourselves
gather our friends
speak in secret languages

emptied onto alien ports
invasive creatures carried
in the ballast of container ships

importing our lives like canned tomatoes
that arrive aboard a ship
across the ocean

we can design a home
in the empty corners of our minds
a tenement room
where street lights flood in
with a sliver of moon

we'll gather in the tight kitchen
play an old record in the basement
sing songs we love
break our hearts
a loaf of bread ripped in two

Passenger

by LITUO HUANG

from *JMWW*

It was the third day. Things had begun to unravel. We'd slept poorly, and both of us had missed our breakfasts and bowel movements. I watched Ripley feel his stubble as he drove, his unwashed hand brushing over the bristles that peppered the broken vessels on his round cheeks. At eleven a.m., the shimmer already rose two feet off the road. The car's A/C was dying, blinking its green and orange lights and spewing air the temperature of a fever.

"Five more miles," Ripley said, reading the sign. This was the first time either of us had spoken in seventy miles, since passing the sign that read *No services next 75 miles.*

"Hurray."

"You can use the little girls' room. Again."

He was trying, but I was tired of jokes. This trip had been meant to repair us. Instead, the space between us had grown into a small, silent ghost.

"Ha ha," I said anyway.

The day before, we'd driven past a length of highway on fire, the flames dancing through holes in the Jersey wall and sending black smoke up to blue-white heaven. We'd driven by mesas backlit by enormous moons. We'd driven on a road scraping out a mountain, revealing layers of sandstone the color of dust, bone, muscle, and blood.

This morning, there was only dry brush dotting a brown field that met the sky at an invisible distance. We passed a single dead jackrabbit on the side of the road. Finally, we bumped down the off-ramp to a run-down Chevron. I sat and waited for Ripley to say something, but he got out and started pumping gas.

"Want anything?" I asked, after a few minutes.

"Nah." He stared at the display with one hand on the pump handle, waiting to pull the trigger on a number that ended in zero.

Inside it wasn't much cooler. I made my way towards the ice freezer that always stood a sentinel to the bathroom. The ancient attendant tried to stop me.

"Running from the Chupacabra?" he asked. The thin brown

skin stretched tight over his skull reminded me of a bog mummy.

He tried again. "Where you headed?"

I closed the bathroom door. I had a secret to nurse.

After I came out, I found the old man talking at Ripley, who had amassed a feast of chips, beef jerky, sunflower seeds, and soda on the counter.

"Rip here says you're headed to Phoenix," said the man, turning on me. There were dirty blue spots in the whites of his eyes.

"*Rip* sure is right about that." I put my arm through Ripley's and gave him a look.

He ignored the look. Asked if I liked the ranch ones.

"Sure, whatever," I said, "Ranch, barbeque, pickle and ice cream." I felt his arm stiffen, and I smiled.

The old man was talking. "Phoenix. Last man here from Phoenix killed himself."

"What?" I pulled on Ripley's arm. He pulled away.

"Ye-as," he continued, "A young man. He stopped here to buy cigarettes. Said he was dying of lung cancer and was driving out here to kill himself. Arranged it all. Kids provided for. Showed me the gun he did it with." The old man looked like the story was delicious in his mouth.

I made a noise. "He showed you his gun?"

The old man kept talking, not looking at either of us now but looking between us. "Planned it all out. Not twenty miles from here. Pulled over and got out and shot himself right through the head, right here." He jabbed at a spot on his own head above the temple with a dry finger.

Ripley wasn't moving, so I took out my wallet and put the money on the counter.

"Great," I said," Thanks."

The old man went on. "And you know what was funny? He didn't even smoke. Cancer came out of nowhere. Genetic vulnerability, he called it. Told me he wanted to try a smoke before the end though. Life's a trip."

"Let's go," I said, shoving the snacks into my purse and yanking Ripley through the door.

In the car, after we'd finished the Cokes and chips, I said, "What an old freak."

Ripley cracked a sunflower seed and flicked the shell out of his window, where the vortex of wind whipped it away.

"Don't you think he was a freak?" I asked again.

The roar of the highway ate his reply.

"How did he even know all that? It makes no sense."

"Police scanner, maybe," Ripley said, with one hand on the wheel and the other out the window, spearing the wind.

"You don't know."

"You're right," he said, with a kind of edge in it, "I don't know."

I felt hot. I had a headache. The sun, filtered through glass, choked me. I said finally, "I thought you weren't hungry."

Ripley made a sucking sound through his teeth, like he did when he'd had enough. So I turned on the radio.

"Turn that off," he said.

I turned it up. Voices of the dead came through static. *Oh baby, oh baby*. Ripley smacked the dial so hard that I jumped, and the seat belt caught.

"I told you to turn that off," he said, "Fuck's sake. Fuck's sake."

We drove in silence to miles of brown earth under a sky turning white. I looked out at the highway lines that were always converging and never meeting. I looked in the side mirror and saw the face of a passenger.

After a while, I put my hand on Ripley's thigh.

"What are you thinking about?"

"Nothing," he said, but I was thinking about a dead jackrabbit, blood in the mountain, and a man with a hole in his head where the wind whistled through, already hollow.

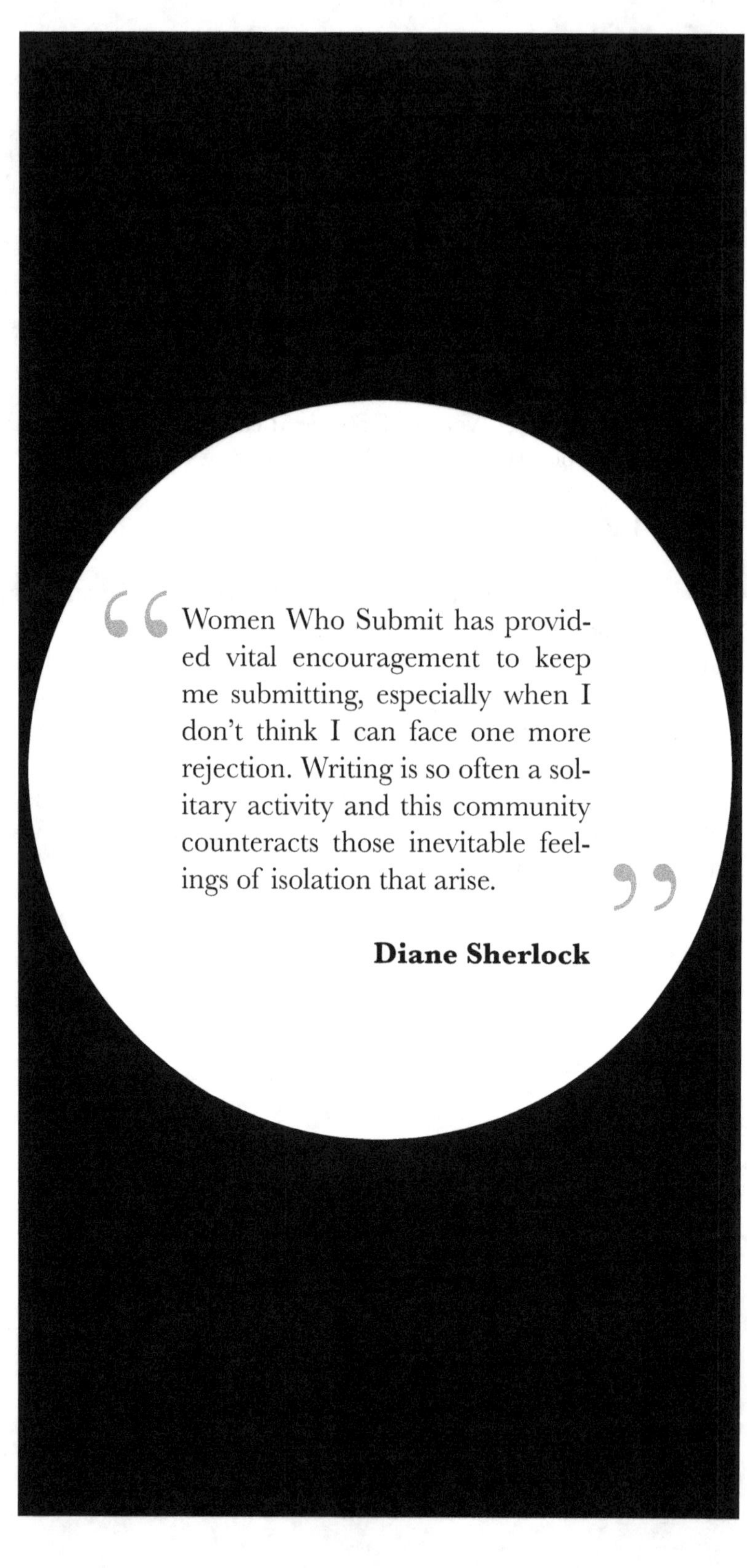
"Women Who Submit has provided vital encouragement to keep me submitting, especially when I don't think I can face one more rejection. Writing is so often a solitary activity and this community counteracts those inevitable feelings of isolation that arise."
Diane Sherlock

CONTRIBUTORS

Li Yun Alvarado is the author of *Words or Water*. Her work has appeared in *VIDA Review*; *The Acentos Review*; and *Aster(ix)*, among others. An alumna of VONA and AROHO. Li Yun grew up in NY, lives in CA, and takes travels to Salinas, PR to see familia.

Jamie Asaye FitzGerald is an L.A.-based poet from Hawaii. Her poems have appeared in *The American Poetry Review*, *Works & Days*, *Mom Egg Review*, and elsewhere. She earned an MFA in poetry from SDSU and a BA in English/Creative Writing from USC where she received an Academy of American Poets College Prize and the Edward Moses Poetry Prize.

Erika Ayón emigrated from Mexico when she was five years old and grew up in South Central Los Angeles. She graduated from UCLA with a B.A. in English. She was selected as a 2009 PEN Emerging Voices Fellow. Her first collection of poetry, *Orange Lady*, was published by World Stage Press.

librecht baker authored *vetiver* (Finishing Line Press). She's an English Professor and Sundress Publications' Assistant Editor. Her play *Taciturn Beings* received a stage reading in The Vagrancy's Blossoming: A New Play Reading Series. Baker participated in Eastside Queer Stories Playwright Festival. Her poetry appears in *Sinister Wisdom 107* and other publications.

Jennifer Barone is the author of *Saporoso, Poems of Italian Food & Love* (FeatherPress), host of the monthly WordParty Poetry & Jazz Series, and two-time winner of the Poets Eleven contest for North Beach where she resides.

When not traveling and birding with her husband, **Cindy Carlson** spends her time along the Chesapeake Bay in Virginia. Winner of the 2016 Hampton Roads Writers contest for creative nonfiction and co-founder of Norfolk's WWS, her work appears in travel journals *The Wayfarer*, *Bird's Thumb*, *hippocampus*, *Barely South*, *Tiferet*, and *Chautauqua*.

Lisa Eve Cheby, a librarian and poet, holds an MFA from Antioch University Los Angeles and an MLIS from SJSU. Her poems and reviews have appeared in various journals and anthologies. Her chapbook, *Love Lessons from Buffy the Vampire Slayer*, is available from Dancing Girl Press.

Lisbeth Coiman is an emerging, bilingual writer who has wandered the immigration path from Venezuela to Canada to the US. In her self-published memoir, *I Asked the Blue Heron*, she explores the intersection between immigration and mental health. She lives in Los Angeles where she works and dances salsa.

Flint is a queer writer, radical feminist, and performance artist with an abiding interest in hybridity, performativity, and generative genre-tampering. Recent publications include *Arts & Letters*, winner of the 2019 Unclassifiable Contest (and the world's first prose villanelle), *NAILED Magazine*, *Bending Genres*, Cathexis Northwest Press, and *Unchaste* Anthology Volume 3.

Sarah Rafael García is a performance ethnographer, author of *Las Niñas* and *SanTana's Fairy Tales*, founder of Barrio Writers and LibroMobile, and a 2019 UH KGMCA-Project Row Houses Fellow. Currently, she splits her time between stacking books in Santa Ana, California and creating a sci-fi literary project in Houston, Texas.

After helping countless students find their voices, **LaCoya Katoe Gessesse** decided to unlock her own, completing courses and workshops with Gotham Writer's Workshop, Northwestern University, and Voices of Our Nation Arts. She has an MFA from Antioch University Los Angeles and continues to facilitate workshops for teens, lectures, and tutors college students at Antioch University Los Angeles.

Cybele Garcia Kohel is a writer living and writing in Pasadena, California. Born in Puerto Rico, she writes through the many lenses provided by her diverse background and the streets of Los Angeles. You can read her work in *Vine Leaves Journal* Issue #15, *These Fragile Lilacs Poetry Journal*, the *Women's Voices Issue*, the *Altadena*

Poetry Review, *New American Legends*, and *Screaming from the Silence Anthology* (Vociferous Press, 2020).

Anita Gill is a teacher and a writer. Winner of the 2018 *Iowa Review* Award in Nonfiction, Anita has humor and essays in *Prairie Schooner*, *McSweeney's Internet Tendency*, *The Rumpus*, *The Iowa Review*, and elsewhere. She will be a Fulbright Fellow to Spain for 2019-2020.

Cynthia Guardado is Salvadorian-American and a Professor of English at Fullerton College. She received her MFA from CSU Fresno and her debut poetry collection, *ENDEAVOR*, was published by World Stage Press (2017). Her second manuscript, *Cenizas*, a collection of poems centered on El Salvador and grief, is currently under review.

Rebecca Gomez Farrell's epic fantasy, *Wings Unseen*, debuted from Meerkat Press in 2017. Her shorter pieces have appeared over twenty times in publications such as *Typehouse Literary Magazine*, *Beneath Ceaseless Skies*, and the *Fright into Flight* anthology from Word Horde. Becca also runs theGourmez.com, a food and drink blog.

Minal Hajratwala wrote *Leaving India: My Family's Journey from Five Villages to Five Continents* (winner of four nonfiction awards), *Bountiful Instructions for Enlightenment*, and the *Moon Fiji* travel guidebook (2019); edited *Out! Stories from the New Queer India*; co-founded The (Great) Indian Poetry Collective; and created Write Like a Unicorn to help writers tap their magic.

Tanya (Hyonhye) Ko Hong is a poet, translator, and cultural curator. She holds an MFA from Antioch University Los Angeles and is a PhD candidate in Mythological Studies at Pacifica Graduate Institute. She is the author of four books, won the Yun Doon-ju Korean-American Literature Award, and was a Pushcart nominee.

Lituo Huang is a Chinese-born, Midwest-bred, Los Angeles-based writer. Her fiction and poetry have previously appeared or are forthcoming in *JMWW*, *Bosie Magazine*, the *Bethlehem Writers Roundtable*, the *Recenter Press Poetry Journal*, and elsewhere.

Toni Ann Johnson's short fiction has appeared in *The Emerson Review*, *Hunger Mountain*, *Callaloo*, and many other publications. Her novel, *Remedy For a Broken Angel* (2014) was nominated for a 2015 NAACP Image Award for Outstanding Literary Work by a Debut

Author. She teaches screenwriting at USC.

Poet **Bonnie S. Kaplan** is a second-generation Angeleno. Kaplan's poems are published in *Adrienne Rich: A Tribute Anthology*, *This Assignment is So Gay: LGBTIQ Poets on the Art of Teaching*, and *Out of Sequence: The Sonnets Remixed.*

Cassandra Lane's stories have appeared in *The New York Times'* "Conception" series, *The Times-Picayune*, *The Atlanta Journal Constitution*, *Writers Resist*, *Everything But the Burden*, *Expressing Motherhood*, The Tennessee Williams Festival, and elsewhere. She is Managing Editor of *L.A. Parent* magazine and serves on the board of the AROHO Foundation.

Muriel Leung is the author of *Bone Confetti*, winner of the 2015 Noemi Press Book Award, and a Pushcart Prize-nominated writer. She received fellowships to Kundiman, VONA/Voices Workshop and Community of Writers. She is the Poetry Co-Editor of *Apogee Journal* and a Dornsife Fellow in Creative Writing and Literature at USC.

Elline Lipkin's first book, *The Errant Thread*, was chosen by Eavan Boland for the Kore Press First Book Award. Her second book, *Girls' Studies*, was published by Seal Press. Research Scholar with UCLA's Center for the Study of Women, she also teaches for Writing Workshops Los Angeles. From 2016-2018, she was Poet Laureate of Altadena.

Sakae Manning's storytelling centers on historical and contemporary alliances, solidarity, and intersectionality amongst women of color. Her work has been in *Carve Magazine*, *Dryland*, and *Making Waves: An Anthology of Asian-American Women Writers*. During her residency at The Annenberg Community Beach House, Manning produced programs featuring women writers of color.

Kate Maruyama's novel *Harrowgate* was published by 47North. Her short work has appeared in numerous journals and anthologies, largely thanks to Women Who Submit. She writes, teaches, cooks, and eats in Los Angeles, where she lives with her family.

Danielle Mitchell's debut chapbook *Makes the Daughter-in-Law Cry* is the winner of the Clockwise Chapbook Prize (Tebot Bach, 2017). Her poems have appeared in *Vinyl*, *Baltimore Review*, *apt*,

Hayden's Ferry Review, and others. Her essays have been featured on DIY MFA, Women Who Submit, and Malahat Review.

Mia Nakaji Monnier is a freelance writer and co-editor of *The Blend*, a HelloGiggles vertical dedicated to mixed-race and multicultural identity. Her essays and journalism have appeared in *The Boston Globe*, BuzzFeed, *The Washington Post*, and more. Previously, she worked on staff at Japanese American community newspaper *The Rafu Shimpo*.

Janel Pineda is a Los Angeles-born poet and daughter of Salvadoran immigrants who fled civil war in 1980. She has performed internationally and been published in anthologies, including *The Wandering Song: Central American Writing in the United States*. Janel holds a BA from Dickinson College, studied at University of Oxford, and is a 2019 Marshall Scholar.

Lisa Richter's stories, poems, and essays have appeared in the *Santa Monica Review*, *Orange Coast Review*, *Squaw Valley Review*, *Months to Years*, and elsewhere. An alumna of the Community of Writers at Squaw Valley, she holds an MFA from Antioch University Los Angeles.

Heather Romero-Kornblum is a San Francisco researcher and writer. Heather has been a featured poet at Mutiny Radio and The WordParty Poetry and Jazz monthly series, Sacred Grounds—the longest running open mic in San Francisco. Under the pen name Heather Korn, she has two novels and three poetry collections.

Sehba Sarwar's writings have appeared in the *New York Times*, *Vallum*, *Creative Times Report*, and elsewhere. Her novel *Black Wings* (second edition) was released in 2019 (Veliz Books). Born and raised in Pakistan in a home filled with artists and activists, Sarwar is a member of the Macondo Writers Workshop.

Arielle Silver's essays, poems, and hybrid misfits have appeared in *Matador Review*, *Brevity*, *Under the Gum Tree*, *Gulf Stream*, *Jet Fuel Review*, *Lilith Magazine*, and others. She teaches at Antioch University Los Angeles, performs as a singer/songwriter in venues nationally, and leads yoga and creativity retreats worldwide.

Leticia Urieta is a proud Tejana writer from Austin, TX, where she works as a teaching artist. She is a graduate of Agnes Scott College and holds an MFA in Fiction writing from Texas State University. Her work appears or is forthcoming in *Cleaver*, *Chicon Street Poets* Anthology, *BorderSenses*, *Lumina*, *The Offing*, *Kweli*, and others.

Romaine Washington is the author of a collection of poems, *Sirens in Her Belly*. She is a facilitator for Inlandia Writing Workshop and a fellow of the Inland Area Writing Project, UC Riverside and The Watering Hole, South Carolina.

Aruni Wijesinghe is a project manager, occasional sous chef, and erstwhile bellydance instructor. She holds a BA in English from UCLA, an AA in dance from Cypress College, and a certification in TESOL from UC Irvine. She is an emerging voice in the Los Angeles and Orange County literary communities.

Hazel Kight Witham is a writer, teacher, activist, artist, and mother of two, whose work can be found in a lovely collection of literary journals. She holds a BA from Brown University and an MFA from Antioch University Los Angeles. As a proud public school teacher, she loves listening to young people and challenging them to think.

Désirée Zamorano is an award-winning short story writer and the author of the critically acclaimed novel *The Amado Women*. Her many publications of essays and short stories include the *Los Angeles Review of Books*, *Cultural Weekly*, *Catapult*, *Huizache*, and *Kenyon Review*.

EDITORS & FOUNDERS

Nonfiction editor **Ryane Nicole Granados** is an AWP featured presenter and has attended the Bread Loaf Writer's Conference in Sicily, Voices of Our Nation Arts, and the Community of Writers at Squaw Valley Workshop. Her storytelling has been showcased in the national stage production Expressing Motherhood and KPCC's Live Series Unheard LA. Her novella *The Aves* is forthcoming. She earned her MFA in Creative Writing from Antioch University Los Angeles.

Nonfiction editor **Noriko Nakada** edits the Breathe and Push column for the WWS blog. Her essay, "A Short History of Insanity," appeared in *Meridian*. She has published two book-length memoirs: *Through Eyes Like Mine*, which was shortlisted for the 2040 Books Award, and *Overdue Apologies*: a middle school memoir. She completed her MFA at Antioch University Los Angeles and teaches English in a Los Angeles public middle school.

Nonfiction editor **Ashley Perez** is one of Women Who Submit's fundraising coordinators. Her primary role is to secure donations for and promote WWS fundraising efforts. She has also presented on submission strategies at the Latina Writers Conference. She runs the literary site Arts Collide and does work of all varieties for Redeemed, Jaded Ibis Press, and Why There Are Words. She holds an MFA in Creative Writing from Antioch University Los Angeles.

Managing and fiction editor **Rachael Warecki** is the webmaster and graphic designer for Women Who Submit. She also facilitates digital methods for making WWS more accessible to writers with disabilities. Her published work has garnered the 2017 *Tiferet* Prize in Fiction, a 2014 Best of the Net nomination, and a 2011 Honorable Mention in *Glimmer Train*'s Short Story Award for New Writers. She holds an MFA from Antioch University Los Angeles, is an alumna of the Tin House Writers' Workshop, and has been awarded residencies at The Wellstone Center and Ragdale.

Managing and fiction editor **Tisha Marie Reichle-Aguilera** is the Facebook curator for Women Who Submit. Her primary role is to compile and schedule calls for submission. She is also a writer for WWS grants. She has presented on submission strategies at Macondo Writers Workshop, the Latina Writers Conference and Antioch University Residency. Her unpublished novel was a finalist for 2040 Books Award. She earned a creative writing MFA from Antioch University Los Angeles and is a PhD student in creative writing and literature at University of Southern California, where she is a Wallis Annenberg Fellow.

Poetry editor **Lauren Eggert-Crowe** is one of Women Who Submit's fundraising coordinators and editor of the Behind The Editor's Desk on the WWS blog. Her primary role is to support and publicize WWS's programming efforts. She has also presented on submission strategies at a UCLA Extension class and has co-presented Women Who Submit history at BinderCon 2016. She is the author of four poetry chapbooks, including *Bitches of the Drought*, which was selected as a finalist in the Sundress Publications 2016 Chapbook Competition. She has an MFA in Poetry from The University of Arizona.

Poetry editor **Xochitl-Julisa Bermejo** is co-founder and Los Angeles headquarters director of Women Who Submit. She serves as WWS's liaison to Exposition Park Branch of the Los Angeles Public Library and other community organizations. She is WWS's primary grant writer. She has presented on submission strategies at Macondo Writers Workshop, Hugo House, BinderCon, and other places. Her poetry collection, *Posada: Offering of Witness and Refuge*, was published by Sundress Publications in 2016. She earned a creative writing MFA from Antioch University Los Angeles and teaches creative writing through UCLA Extension, Antioch University, and Writing Workshops LA; she is also a community arts educator.

Alyss Dixson is co-founder of Women Who Submit. She studied at Yale, Columbia, and San Francisco State. She is the 2015 recipient of the Joseph Henry Jackson Award from the San Francisco Foundation, a graduate Fellow of Cave Canem Foundation, a Callaloo Creative Writing Workshop, Poetry Fellow and a Visiting Scholar-Artist in Residence at The Ohio State University.

Dr. Ashaki M. Jackson is co-founder and chapters director of Women Who Submit. Her primary role is facilitating chapter orientations online and communicating with chapter leads. She has presented on submission strategies for Lambda Literary, the Mixed Remixed Festival, and the Association of Writers and Writing Programs (AWP) conference. She is an alumna of Cave Canem and VONA. She earned a creative writing MFA from Antioch University Los Angeles and a psychology doctorate from Claremont Graduate University.

www.ingramcontent.com/pod-product-compliance
Lightning Source LLC
Chambersburg PA
CBHW071522100726
47908CB00004B/1267

* 9 7 8 1 7 3 3 2 4 1 5 2 6 *